Zoom88

How to be calmer and improve your music making

Rosemary Wiseman

Published by New Generation Publishing in 2019

First Edition

ISBN: 978-1-78955-352-9

www.newgeneration-publishing.com

New Generation Publishing

Dedications

For my students, who inspired me to keep going with this book and without whom it could not have been written.

Dedicated to Judy Gabriel, of whose violin and piano teaching ideas I would like to have known even more about.

Dr Roger Callahan – Music meets TFT tapping.
Josie, your message will live on through *Zoom88*.

Rosemary's students and some of their parents, comment on the writing of *Zoom88.*

"I'll read it because I'm not good with performing and it would help me deal with that and improve my skills."

"It will help others without you being there. They will feel more relaxed when they know what to do."

"It will be helpful to many people. They will enjoy it, as it's about lots of different techniques and opinions of different students."

"You are an experienced music teacher and have different techniques that I have seen you helping with, like the tapping and breathing work, so this book will be useful."

"You obviously have a fairly idiosyncratic way of teaching. I am interested to read the book to see how you got there. What you have learned to make you the teacher you are."

"I love books. People will get to know how you teach. 'Today we are going to do something special' you said. Every lesson is different with you, like a box of chocolates."

"People build up nerves and unnecessary blocks. You have the ability to make people concentrate and take away needless pressure. It is an amazing contribution to the music world."

"It helps with confidence in life. I can see *Zoom88* works. You are writing from practical experience, based on working with your students."

"It will be helpful, as if someone is not your student, you can still help them in another way."

"Your students and readers will benefit a lot from it."

"So inspiring. Not many other music teachers would do this to help students achieve their potential. You give a lot of support and are very encouraging, almost as if you are going through it yourself. If you can reach out and show others these techniques to achieve performing how they want, it will be great, for all ages. People get anxious performing. You are equipping them with skills to manage this."

"It will help lots of people to be more confident when teaching."

"I think it's going to be interesting, as I haven't read any book like it. It's a good idea because students are 'self-taught' in between lessons and they get stuck. This book would help them to know what to do."

"It will be really good for beginners to be confident with their instrument; also for someone really into music. They will learn things they have not learned before and improve what they are doing, for example: the *musical secretary*."

"It's a good idea. I've been coming to you a long time and I'm quite good at the piano, so presumably you've got quite a lot to share."

Music teachers' comments on reading drafts of *Zoom88*

"Often students do not practice, the teacher is then left with the dilemma: how do I get them to 'Grade 1'? The objective becomes 'the exam' and with this in mind the teacher uses short cuts or whichever methods they can to get them there as quickly as possible.

This book will give ideas to help students get on with practising, as well as how to practise; a music handbook of the future."
- Lewis, clarinet and saxophone teacher

"As I read I kept saying, 'this is my life experience.'
It was so involving, so helpful. I found in the book what I am learning about in my Suzuki training. The music lesson on pleasure is pure Suzuki. I loved the *successipe* as Suzuki's phrase is 'success breeds success.' "

"I found your book really interesting and inspiring, making me think of why and how we do things as teachers and students ourselves. The philosophy of putting yourself in your pupil's shoes to understand difficulties and creative ways to overcome these mirrors Suzuki's, with the concept that 'every child can' when nurtured in the right way. Building blocks from a firm foundation are like your staircase."

"My thoughts on hearing about TFT tapping were that I was open to finding out more - as a medic I know people often make assumptions that only classical ways are correct, but what I have gathered so far very much links into ancient Chinese medicine which predates a lot of western approaches and so needs to be embraced, even if people do not subscribe to the ideas about energy channels and so on."
- Alyson, Suzuki recorder teacher

"I found your book absorbing, very enjoyable and informative."
- Sandra, piano teacher

Foreword

It was in 2004 that I first heard from Rosemary Wiseman. She emailed me an article: "Brief notes on Music Students helped by Thought Field Therapy (TFT)." With my background in music, psychology and TFT, I was intrigued and excited by how Rosemary had begun using TFT to help her students learn and perform with more ease, precision, and joy.

Included in Rosemary's notes was how she was using TFT to correct, through simple tapping techniques, problems with pitch, rhythm, sight-reading, finger agility and more. She was helping remove students' frustration, guilt, embarrassment, anxiety, anger, fear and trauma, which are often associated with - and get in the way of - learning, practising, performing and taking music exams. Rosemary's conclusion at the end of her notes was that, *"through using TFT to correct problems in musical performance, the potential of the musician can be realised and in so doing, their emotional and physical health, together with their academic ability can also improve, as well as their musical performance!"*

What is this powerful method? TFT is a safe, effective, self-help technique that involves tapping energy meridian points in a specific order to eliminate problems that keep us from functioning at an optimal level. This fundamental healing code was discovered and developed by the brilliant psychologist, Dr. Roger Callahan, about whom you can read more in Chapter 34.

Shortly after my email introduction to Rosemary, I began working with her and some of her students as a TFT consultant. Because I had been trained by Dr. Callahan at the most advanced level of TFT, "Voice Technology" (VT), I could determine causes and appropriate corrections over the phone. We would arrange phone consultations during some of her music lessons, and I would help with more complex cases. It was highly rewarding to work with such a professional, creative, and compassionate music teacher as Rosemary. And it was a joy hearing how students were benefitting from our collaboration.

Music had been my first passion in life. My youth revolved around piano lessons, accompanying and singing in musicals and choirs, and singing and recording with a trio. I majored in Music in college, and then went on to receive a Master's degree in Educational Psychology, for which my thesis was a guide to teaching music in pre-school. I know the deep joy music can bring to one's life. We are drawn to music because it touches us in a way nothing else does. Through music we can reach the depths of our being. But things can get in the way of this magical experience - frustration, anxiety, fear, traumatic memories, confusion, to name a few.

For me to be able to help Rosemary free students to feel at ease with and truly enjoy their musical experience, was a real gift to me. And now, *this gift is in your hands*, honed by fifteen more years of Rosemary's experience, creativity, and dedication. It is rich with discovery, experience, wisdom, and good humour.

In the first part of *Zoom88*, Rosemary generously shares her musical journey - how her own anxieties spurred her on to find ways to deal with them and in so doing, help others. How her challenges shaped her to be the gifted and committed teacher and performer that she is. Rosemary's life exemplifies how the closing of one door leads to the opening of another.

Part 2 of *Zoom88* is a virtual recipe book of ideas and practical tips for learning, practising, performing and even being tested in music. (I can only imagine the hundreds of hours applying these tips would have saved me in practice!) Rosemary is playful in her approach and even the youngest of children will appreciate and enjoy these tips, which are often in game form.

Part 2 could have been a music student or teacher's guide book in and of itself, but what about the student whose thoughts or emotional upsets get in the way of his learning or performing? What about the student who, no matter how hard she tries or practises, just cannot get the rhythm or the notes right, or cannot memorise music, or sight-read? Stories of students with challenges such as these are described in Part 3, along with how Rosemary's use of TFT eliminated the challenges, thereby transforming the students' musical experience. This part is what makes *Zoom88* so very unique. It offers an entirely new possibility and opportunity for opening one's full musical potential and enjoyment.

And how about you? Might there be anything in the way of your own truly fun, relaxed, fulfilling musical practice, performance, or exam taking? *Zoom88* does not end with stories about others. It also describes how YOU can use these easy techniques to enhance your own experience with music - and other areas of your life as well.

I truly believe that *Zoom88* is an extraordinarily effective and powerful resource for music students and teachers and should be read and referred to often. *Enjoy your read. May it open you to an ever more fun, wondrous world of music.*

Mary Cowley

Mary L. Cowley, PhD, TFT-VT
Virginia, USA
A Founding Director and Officer of the TFT Foundation, 2003-2017

Contents

Acknowledgements

When I set out to write this book my good friend Michele Ben Moshe, knowing how busy I was already, wondered how I would do this.

Well, it was with a lot of encouragement, the help and patience - after use of TFT tapping - of my friend Kevin Desmond and tracking time spent with my Weekly Rhythm Record, from disciplines taught to me in my own music and business practice and applying it to book writing.

My thanks to Kevin Desmond, for believing in me and for the vision he shared with me of seeing this book completed, as he was helping me along with it; for his amazing use of the TFT tapping and inspiring me to further my own use of this powerful technique. From starting out with title of 'ghost writer,' he became my writing coach, personal literary trainer, writing mentor and 'sounding board'.

I would like to thank the following people for helping me in a variety of ways to get where I am now and for enabling me to have written this book:

Dr Richard Bandler, Dr Colin Barron, Michele Ben Moshe, Eva Bernathova, Michael Beynon, Elizabeth Bourne, Audrey Brain, Stephen Brooks, Sharon Broughall, David Burman, Dr Roger Callahan, Joanne Callahan, Maryse Chomé, Mrs Eileen Cobb (née Downer), Jo Cooper, Carolyn Davidov, Miss Dorothy Davis, Alex Desmond, Sydney Fixman, Mick Goldman, Lorna Gordon, Ian Graham, Miss Gwendoline Harries, Ursula Hess, Leslie Hillman, Rabbi Dr Andrew Kampfner, Barbara Lancaster, Mervyn Leviton, Chaim Lipshitz, Graham Lyons, Caroline Maguire, Hugh Maguire and all the musicians who helped and inspired me along the way, Sara Manasseh, Paul McKenna, Daphne Meek, Helena Meek, Susan Moss, Marios Papadoupolos, Dr Brian Roet, Ronald Singer, Chani Smith, Molly-Ann Smith, Brian Snary, Marion Stone, John Sugarman, Jo Wagerman, Raphael Wallfisch, Michael Webber, Mark Wigglesworth, Miss Zareen.

I would also like to thank my clients and all those who have inspired me to write *Zoom88;* I thank all those who have helped me with the manuscript.

Lastly and above all, I thank my family, without you this book would not have been written: My husband Laurence, our children: David and Natalie Wiseman, my parents: Josie and Sam Woolf, my siblings: Marilynne Adelman, Vivienne Metliss and Bernard Woolf. The opening of doors and references to *An Open Mind* are a tribute to my grandmother, Bessie Marks, who in some ways helped from beyond this world. Thank you Gran.

Prelude

Picture the scene – the past:

A teenager having a piano lesson with their teacher rapping them over the knuckles.

This was my Grandmother and a number of people who I have helped more recently.

Fortunately, my story and those of many others I have come to know has been very different.

Forward to the present:

A student having a piano lesson: the teacher observes patiently as the student calms themselves down using a finger - tapping technique known as Thought Field Therapy (TFT), developed by the clinical psychologist Dr. Roger Callahan.

The inspiration for this book came long before I knew that TFT could help improve musical performance. I wrote down what I was discovering in my music teaching. As I did so, I told many of my students about the emerging book.

When I took the Thought Field Therapy (TFT) diagnostic training course in 2004, it was suggested to me that I write a self-help book on TFT and music. Many people from different walks of life began suggesting I write a book. The subject kept changing. So which one should I actually write?

After attending an introductory course on book writing, my husband Laurence suggested I choose 'the music book'.

Eventually, something happened that made me decide to put my notes and dreams into action. I spoke to a successful businessman who told me why he was so motivated to achieve. He then looked at me directly and asked me what 'my reason why' was. I unconsciously said it was to write a book. That conversation stuck with me and I was just waiting for the 'right time' to begin in earnest.

That time came in November 2013 when something else happened that made me realise I could not wait any longer. I met up with an old friend who I had known since playing in a youth orchestra together. We began chatting about how she had moved from a career in music and was now involved in air racing and competition air rally flying. I was fascinated. How had this begun? "As a dream" she replied. After a short interruption, my friend looked at me in the same way that the businessman had done, as she asked me, "What do *you* really want to do?" Once again the answer came unconsciously - "write a book about what I do, so that students at music colleges and other musicians can find out about the amazing techniques I have come across."

A few days later, I googled my friend - author Kevin Desmond. The door to Kevin and my serious book writing was opened when, to my amazement, I got an email reply on the 18th November 2013: 'Nice to hear from you after so long…how can I help you?' Following this was a voicemail: "This is Kevin Desmond from times past, Willesden and things and vegetarian dogs, et cetera…"

Some wonderful discussions took place over the phone to help get the essence of *Zoom88* on its way. I wrote as quickly as possible as I took notes of the ideas that flowed between us. The day that Kevin innocently suggested 'your autobiography,' that was it; *Zoom88* turned from what could have just been a 'recipe book' about my teaching ideas and music students helped by using TFT tapping, into so much more. He did not know about the journals I had kept, until I started this part of my book. Once I began to write what turned into my musical autobiography, I became unstoppable.

In short, it became an autobiographical adventure, as I began to share the path of my own musical career. It was a journey of discovery at times, and it certainly helped to make sense of my musical life so far.

I came to be grateful for the 'reams' that I had written in my journal, which helped so much in the writing of the early chapters. I found much written evidence of the pleasure I had obtained from my music making and musical experiences. I was keen to put this back into the music profession and give this to others.

All the time Kevin and I were both itching to get to the next practical part of the book, which was developing as I wrote. Still, he encouraged me to pursue and complete my autobiography. At the least I knew it would answer some of the many questions that I began to be asked: "Why did you become a Hypnotherapist?" "What made you decide not to concentrate on just one instrument?" "How did you influence your children and what are they doing now?"

My first working title of this book, *Music All the Way,* began to take on a whole new meaning as my 'recipe book' expanded into *Zoom88.*

Many authors, in their introduction, or even throughout a book, will describe the challenges of writing it. I can add some very 21st century experiences of this. Shortly after I began to prepare the manuscript for *Zoom88,* I lost our hard drive, where much material I had collected over time was stored.

Then there were the other challenges of keeping focused with the daily distractions of life.

Meanwhile, as you will read later in Kevin's chapter, *From Typing to Tapping,* it was inspiring to know that my book project was already having such benefit; Kevin has used TFT tapping so well, both for himself and others.

'You've done wonders in helping Kevin with the tapping – he is so much more relaxed now and much more like his old self! Thank you!' (email to author from his wife Alex Desmond 8th November 2014.)

It was powerful feedback. If *Zoom88* could help one person and many others from that person in this way, I realised that my 'ship must leave the harbour' and this book needed to be read by musicians and others interested in improving their lives.

Over time, when a new idea or lesson was developed, I told my music students that they would be part of my book: "When you read it you can remember 'that was me, it happened in my lesson'." From 2014 I was able to read a few of them some draft chapters or extracts…it was becoming 'real'.

Much as I love short, slim books, *Zoom88* turned out to be much larger than I first thought it would be. Apart from learning a musical instrument, writing it has been the longest project I have ever undertaken and has been like piecing one huge musical jigsaw together. Perhaps music has helped me in this respect.

My vision for this book is that it will help us all to get more enjoyment and pleasure from music making.

Enjoy Zoom88!
Rosemary

ZOOM 1

My musical journey

Chapter 1
Legato or slurred?

The need for an open mind
A Music Exam Centre in North London:
"It went just like you said it would. You did everything to prepare me. It was as if you had been the examiner." A smiling, proud Josie, my Mum, aged 86, had just come back into the waiting room, having completed her first piano exam.

Unfortunately, such a positive experience when completing a music exam is not always the case. Music exam and performance traumas occur all too often. And so often, the reasons for such traumas can be avoided.

Sometimes it's the atmosphere in that waiting room. People whisper or talk in undertones. A nervous mother tells her son, "Are you *absolutely sure* you have got all your music with you?" Another, trying to reassure her trembling violinist daughter says, "Don't worry. It'll be fine." In reality that mother is more nervous than her candidate daughter.

I shall never forget the time when, quite by surprise, my piano teacher Brian Snary "flew in", as he described it and turned up at the grade 3 piano exam I was taking at the Royal College of Music. What a relief! Here was another familiar human being beside me in those strange, dark, cold surroundings.

Music exam waiting rooms can sometimes feel like a dentist's waiting room, although in most cases without the proverbial tropical fish tank. You really have to be prepared for anything when you enter such a room.

It is rare that a music examiner will set a candidate's mind at ease by coming out and welcoming them, although I have seen it done a few times. One examiner even gave the young candidate a 'high five' as it was her birthday that day!

So, as a piano accompanist, the challenge for me is to help candidates to feel as comfortable as possible.

Take the case of Richard, a French horn player. It seemed to be quite an ordinary morning as I sat in this particular music exam waiting room in Harrow, North West London. This was part of a house being used as an exam centre. Alison, the Grade 3 flute candidate I was accompanying, had turned up on time and her instrument, on this occasion, was in full working order.

We waited for the previous exam to finish. This period, before Alison would be blowing away all the adrenalin and nervous excitement through her flute, was a highly sensitive moment; all anyone really wants to see is the previous candidate come out smiling and saying, "The examiner was really nice."

Some candidates need to "warm up" while others, or their parents, need to "calm down".

That day, my support in this respect risked being reduced to nothing. Suddenly our hushed silence was broken by an outburst from Richard's mother, as she saw her teenage son rushing out of the exam room, then through the front door of the house and out into the street.

Indeed, he refused to come back into the house, let alone the exam room. Both mother and instrumental teacher were unable to persuade him to return.

For anyone who understands the pressures that music examiners are under to complete the exam in the required number of minutes, this was a tense situation for all concerned.

Due to the unusual demand for some flexibility in these circumstances, the examiner kindly suggested that he would be happy to re-examine Richard *after* my candidate had taken her flute exam.

This was my 'green light'. I felt I just had to do something to help this young man get back into the house, the exam room, or at least a safe place. It was a gut reaction: to help out when no one else could.

I found Richard, with his French horn, standing in the road trying to get into a car! Had he been old enough, I think he would have driven himself away from the scene.

Fortunately, he was blessed with enough of an open mind to learn something new, as most children and young people are, so he accepted my offer of help.

I managed to encourage him to return to the house and then into the privacy of an adjoining room. I then guided the traumatised teenager through tapping a few specific sequences of Thought Field Therapy (TFT)[1] to eliminate his distress.

Often, just one tapping sequence would have calmed his emotions. Yet for Richard I quickly realised this was not the case and that this was not going to be as simple as I had first thought. We only had a few minutes before he had to go back into that exam room. Fortunately, following the TFT tapping, he was at least able to calm down enough to tell me what had happened in his first exam attempt.

He told me that in the scales section, he had been asked to play a scale "slurred". As he had been taught that the word for playing smoothly was "legato", he did not understand what the examiner was asking for when he said, "slurred". In addition to this confusion and to make things worse, Richard got the impression that the examiner was laughing at him.

This was in 2005, before the instructions given by music examiners, such as the terms they use, had been standardised. Today, in the ABRSM aural test, there is a printed 'rubric' in the practice test books, which the examiner must present to each candidate. This enables them to become completely familiar with what is expected and the instructions they will receive on the day of their exam. At the time of writing, there is still no similar 'rubric' for the scales.

In the end, my brief interaction with Richard lasted only a matter of minutes. This was the time during which Alison, my Grade 3 candidate, was completing her own exam.

Richard was then able to go back into the exam room and resume his French horn exam. I later heard from him that he got a Pass of 107 marks (100 being the pass mark).

Richard's case is just one example of the way in which I have been able to help people to prepare for an exam, an audition or a concert, simply by demonstrating techniques using my fingertips. It is my goal to share these amazing tapping techniques and the discoveries I have made through them, with as many people as possible.

Later on, I will be sharing some of those very varied experiences with you. Let me begin by telling you about the crucial formative years which led up to my being able to help Richard and so many anxious people like him.

---

[1] The procedures of Thought Field Therapy TFT are explained in the Appendix.

Chapter 2
All the way back to my childhood
1956-1974

My ability to help traumatised or anxious musicians to get the best out of their musical performance goes back to my early childhood.

I was born in London in 1956, the youngest of four children. We lived in a large detached house in Aylestone Avenue, opposite what was then called Aylestone School, now Queens Park Community School, in Willesden.

Looking back now, I realise that everything and everybody, in one way or another, paved the way for my musical career.

When my parents, Josie and Sam Woolf, bought our house, it came with a beautiful Challen grand piano, which stood proudly in the bay window of our lounge.

One of my earliest memories was being taken in the family pram to my sisters' piano lessons. They were taught by a lady called Sheila Beckensall. Sheila was also a violinist with the London Philharmonic Orchestra (LPO). Years later I would go with my mother and see Sheila perform in concerts at the Royal Festival Hall. There were very few women orchestral players at that time.

My own musical talent was first spotted when I was only three years old. I sang the whole of my cousin's Bar Mitzvah in Hebrew before I could even read a word of that language.

Of course, I wanted everything that my older siblings had. When my brother Bernard was given a new pair of sandals, I had to have some too! So perhaps it was quite natural for me to want piano lessons.

Despite my nagging, I remember being told I could only start to learn the piano when I could read, a common belief in those days.

My own piano lessons began at the age of seven. I was introduced to the piano by a Miss Gwendoline Harries, who was already teaching my sister Vivienne. Giggling with my big sister in Miss Harries's cosy dark front room created a relaxed atmosphere; something I have since found important.

4

Sadly, when my Grandmother was a teenager and attempting to learn the piano, the atmosphere was far from relaxed. Indeed, the teacher rapped her on her knuckles with a long pencil to make her curve her fingers, causing an abrupt end to her musical career.

And yet, imagine my reaction when our teacher once told me that I was playing "like a cart horse!" Teachers, please be careful of comments made to students!

Almost prophetically, one of the first pieces I learned was about a water tap. I can still recall the picture of the tap in my music book and the words, 'Drip drop drip drop all the night, I forgot to turn it tight.'

Taking it in turns with my sister, I would regularly practise our piano, often with our little dog Sally on the end of the long stool for company. While on one side of the room there was a lovely view onto our back garden, from the other I often had to compete against the noise of children in the playground of Aylestone School. As if that were not enough, there was the distinctive sound of tapping coming from the school's steel band.

And then there was our neighbour, a professional opera singer. As the bathroom of her house was situated closest to my bedroom window, I would often be woken up by her practising her vocal exercises in the bath. She also had a spacious and elegant music room downstairs with a harp in it.

Despite all these distractions, I pressed on.

When Miss Harries sadly passed away, this might have marked the end of piano lessons for me, as it had done for Vivienne. Fortunately, a year later, I was able to resume my lessons with a Miss Zareen, who would sit beside me at the piano and play everything that I was playing, a few octaves higher.

At Malorees Junior School in Willesden, I found myself in the same class as Caroline Maguire, daughter of the well-known Irish violinist Hugh Maguire, who was then leader of the London Symphony Orchestra. Indeed, the first concert I ever attended was to hear him perform - an unforgettable experience.

Mrs Cobb, our class and recorder teacher, and also the headmaster Mr Singer, were both very keen on music. Every time Hugh Maguire was on the BBC Radio, our school lessons would be interrupted so we could tune in.

One morning, when I was about ten years old, we were given a talk by a lady who encouraged us to write our own book. I immediately took up the challenge. Although it was only two and a half pages of fiction, I now proudly felt that I was an author! Alongside my music, I had found my other passion – writing.

Through Mrs Cobb, I began to take part in local music festivals, playing the recorder; our recorder group became the 'music champs' of a number of these. So began my love of performing and sharing my music with others.

I soon organised my first concert at home in our lounge, even charging my parents an entry fee of a penny. I was happy to take any opportunity to perform. I even played my Grade 1 piano piece, 'The Swing', to our appreciative builder, although he must have already heard it over and over as I had been practising it while he worked around the house.

Indeed, I was fortunate to gain such positive early experiences of performing. This is something I have only come to fully appreciate after hearing some of the less happy, negative experiences of musicians and of my music clients whom I have helped since.

My Uncle Mick played the piano by ear and encouraged me with my piano playing. His daughter, my cousin Patty, used to play *Fur Elise* by Beethoven on the piano. From that moment my father loved this piece. Imagine his joy when in time I too was able to play it as well. The piece has become a family favourite, even with my mother learning it in her eighties.

The only other musicians I knew of in my wider family were my Aunty Helena and her daughter, singer Daphne Meek. A family gathering, festival or meal would always end up with some live music making.

Aunty Helena, my first piano accompanist and two-piano duet partner, as a concert pianist, had given her debut recital at the Wigmore Hall, London. In those days programmes were very long. After the concert, which she had found rather stressful, Aunty Helena decided that she would prefer to play and make music only for pleasure. Until the end of her long life, Helena always enjoyed learning new music.

In the years that have followed, I have adopted her attitude of making sure both I and those I teach get pleasure from making music. Indeed, one of my adult piano students actually called this a 'pleasurometer'.

At my senior school, the Jewish Free School (JFS), my form teachers were also music teachers and they were to have a considerable part to play in my musical life.

On entering JFS I had asked to learn the flute, if perhaps only because it had been recommended to me as a natural progression from the recorder. However, Brian Snary, the new Head of Music, needed a *cellist* in the school orchestra he was assembling; this is how I ended up learning the cello.

My first cello teacher was Miss Dorothy Davis, a very sweet, gentle and quite elderly lady. Each week we would meet in one of those practice or teaching rooms behind the school stage. She guided me along from grade to grade. I only used to practise a few days before my exams, as tuning that awful school cello I rented was such a pain. Of course, Miss Davis was never aware of my lack of practice!

It was through the JFS school orchestra that I came to make some very special musical friends. One of these was my piano and violinist friend Judy Hutter (later Mrs Gabriel), to whom this book is dedicated.

Judy was one year above me at JFS. A wonderful thing about music is how it brings people together, whatever their age.

In the years that followed, despite being separated by distance, Judy and I were to share our very different journeys of becoming professional musicians, music teachers and parents.

Another friend in the JFS school orchestra was a cellist. Unknown to our conductor, Brian Snary, through her influence we would mischievously 'un-tune' our cellos before the rehearsal began, so as to make sure we had less playing time! That is how un-serious I was about my music making on the cello.

Alongside my music, I continued to write. In 1968, just into my second term at JFS, my sister Marilynne gave me the idea to write a diary. Thanks to this little red book and later journals, I have been better able to narrate this part of my book.

In these journals I would write about my musical experiences, showing how I came to manage my nerves through the different stages of my career.

Here for example is one of my very first entries: "*I am quite a lot nervous about tomorrow. Daddy does not know I am playing the cello.*" This was just before my first humiliating public performance on the cello, aged eleven. It might have given anyone else stage fright. Not me.

My father tended to be rather pessimistic and critical, always focusing on my mistakes. That was until his later years when his appreciation of my music making was *only* positive. On the other hand, since my very first musical notes, my mother was always positive about my performances!

It seemed that musical stage fright and real performance nerves were reserved for my school friends.

My mother always reminded me with some interest and amusement about the dreadful state of one of my school friends, just before a concert. Even though they were just singing in the school choir and not a soloist like me, they were a bag of nerves.

In truth, I felt I had been learning the cello for far too short a time - it was only a few weeks – to be performing in a concert to parents in the big school hall. Yet despite my reservations, I loyally agreed with Brian Snary to brave that awe-inspiring high stage.

So, what did happen on that snowy winter's night when my cello teacher Miss Davis would not risk the icy roads in Hampstead to be with me in my hour of need? First, there was me wishing I too lived in Hampstead. Then slowly, as the sound of my short melody progressed and resonated in the packed hall, my cello went more and more out of tune. Then on the final note a string went BANG and snapped!

As if this wasn't enough, I then dropped my cello as I stormed off stage, cursing Mr Snary saying, "I *told* you I shouldn't have played!"

"*We made fools of ourselves*," I wrote later in my journal.

Clearly, I had not been inoculated that breaking a string during a performance *could* occur and had done so even with the most famous of musicians; the greatest virtuoso violinist of the twentieth century, Jascha Heifetz, even injured himself in this way.

Although I was an average height for my age, for some years after that performance I had to put up with people teasing me that "the cello is bigger than you." And yet perhaps it made the biggest impact, as former fellow JFS students still mostly recall that the instrument I played at school was the cello.

My real entertaining career began with concerts at residential homes, performing on the recorder and singing with the JFS school choir with choirmaster, Chaim Lipshitz.

Once again, my recorder-playing partner shook with fear at our performances. Not me. I just quickly learned that one could not giggle and play the recorder at the same time. Perhaps my laughter prevented my suffering from the nerves others had in their teens.

This awareness of the extreme nerves of other performers rather than of my own, was something that would lay the foundations for the future of my helping other musicians and music students, in particular those suffering from anxiety.

When I began JFS as a student, I was really entering the golden years of music making at that school. Gone, I recently found out, were the fearful days of the previous head of music. My music teachers were all very kind, enthusiastic, helpful and encouraging.

Choir rehearsals with Chaim Lipshitz were, for example, a very relaxed experience. As I sat in rehearsals in the clubroom overlooking the much loved school swimming pool, I observed the very simple chordal accompaniments he used.

Later, out of school, with me on the cello and Chaim Lipshitz on the piano, he introduced me to the joys of playing chamber music.

Then there was Brian Snary's inspiring piano performance of Debussy's *Golliwog's Cakewalk*; or the famous photo taken in June 1970 of him with the school choir on their way to perform at the Dorchester Hotel for the United Synagogue centenary celebrations in the presence of Her Majesty the Queen.

I enjoyed the experience, though just why I was only a *reserve* and was denied the opportunity of singing for the Queen, I will never know. At least I was included when she and Prince Philip came over and congratulated us afterwards. At only one and a half metres away, this was the closest I have ever been to our Monarch.

I was devastated when I found out that Mr Snary, who was also my piano teacher, was to leave the school. Seeing my distress that evening after I told my Grandmother, "That is the end of my music," she comforted me with a great 'reframe':

"When one door closes, another opens."

"Will that door open?" I expressed my doubt in my journal, after Brian Snary had said: "You are not God's gift to pianists, yet you are not useless."

I soon found out how right my Grandmother was, for that is exactly what did happen.

That big door was about to open.

It happened one Tuesday morning before school on 27th October 1970. I was playing in and leading a recorder group, run by Chaim Lipshitz. We were in a classroom near the office of the Head of Ivrit (Modern Hebrew studies), Rabbi Dr Andrew Kampfner. I was sitting at the back of the room when Dr Kampfner burst in and asked:

"Who was that playing the recorder so well?"

This was the moment when I was *'discovered'*. Dr Kampfner read the article about me that had just been published in our local newspaper (see photo) and told me he had a friend, a world famous pianist, who might be prepared to teach me. He had no idea that I had been learning the piano with Brian Snary or that I was looking for a new piano teacher.

It was so simple. Dr Kampfner gave me the name and telephone number of Eva Bernathova, a Czech concert pianist and senior lecturer at Trinity College of Music (now called Trinity Laban Conservatoire of Music and Dance); he then suggested I call her. It was a call that changed my life.

Dr Kampfner had known Eva from after the war. He had also known her husband Joseph since they were in Auschwitz concentration camp together. They had lost touch since 1948. It was only through the advertisement for Eva's performance at the Royal Albert Hall in 1968, when she came to live in London, that he made contact once again. It was so fortuitous for me that he did this.

Dr Kampfner proved to have a big influence on me in many ways. He once said to me:

"Rosemary, you need to blow your own trumpet."

Strangely though, it was only many years later that these words were to come in useful, when I became self-employed and was developing my passion for the work I was doing. Up until then everything seemed predestined, from the musical instruments I would learn to play, the people I would meet, to the jobs or work I would find.

On the 21st of December 1970, Brian Snary wrote to my mother:

"I do hope Rosemary keeps working hard at all aspects of her music and I'm sure she will be an asset to the musical profession. I hope I have been of some assistance putting music in her way – it is my life and I hope she makes it hers."

Very optimistically, my mother began to pay for my piano lessons with Eva Bernathova out of her housekeeping money. Finances were not easy, because at this time our family business, M. Woolf Furniture Ltd, of which I was so proud, was beginning to have financial difficulties.

Those piano lessons soon turned out to be a very good investment. Even my mother was benefiting from my more serious interest in music; I noticed how she was listening to more and more music while at her beloved kitchen sink.

For the next nine years, I learned piano with Eva. My initial tears and bewilderment in matching up to her demanding and excellent standards proved well worth it. The foundation of her teaching, regarding how best to practise, will be revealed later in this book.

'Dr Eva', as I once called her in my journal, was to have a big influence on my life. Dr Kampfner once claimed that when he closed his eyes he could hear "the rhythm of Eva Bernathova" in my piano playing.

She taught me far more than the piano. For example, once when we were discussing how I could fit in more piano practice, she suggested I "sleep for half an hour less". I have since found that tip most helpful for many things, such as completing this book!

Eva even suggested I go for walks – not to get to anywhere specific. It was just one of her ways of helping me to relax.

Just as I called her 'Dr Eva', how interesting it is that later one of my own students would call me 'Dr Rosemary', while another student made similar comments about his lessons with me: "That was more than just a music lesson!"

Another door was to open when David Burman took over as Head of Music and my form Tutor at JFS.

I believe my love of playing many instruments came from Dave Burman. Somehow, my dream of learning the flute would not leave me. At his suggestion I took up the instrument at JFS, aged fourteen, in February 1971 with Marion Stone. She was a very good teacher and I was very determined.

Even so, the flute clearly did not come naturally to me. Sitting on my bed, it took me a whole day, on and off, to produce a single sound on just the head joint of that flute! Again, I was unaware at the time that for some students this could take up to five weeks or in some more rare cases, a few months.

Still, I progressed quickly and enjoyed playing in the school wind band. I was surely learning about the powerful effect of music when I reflected on a band rehearsal in my journal that I:

"Really was in a hypnotised mood."

Some days later, on 6th November 1971 I wrote:

"Gave Dad his first piano (my first teaching seriously) lesson. Was not sure whether words would come easily, but they did."

My father was my first and seemingly impossible piano student. However, he would not practise. Whatever I asked him to do, he did it 'his way'. Even though I refused to teach him because of this and we stopped the formal lessons, I encouraged him to pursue his love of music with his piano playing right up to the last year of his life, aged ninety. He would pick out parts of well-known tunes and make up music on the keyboard, giving him a great occupation.

Michael Webber was my housemaster at JFS as I was in Brodetsky House. He was also Head of Art. Although sadly he did not teach me this subject, I do wonder what he would have thought of my love of doodling.

As he did for many others, Michael Webber soon became my friend and mentor. As well as being very dedicated to art, Michael was also very passionate about music and promoted concerts at, for example, London's South Bank. It was at such a concert at the Royal Festival Hall that he jokingly, yet encouragingly, told me that I was like a "one-man band."

Despite his encouragement, I soon came to realise that I really could not play both the cello and flute in the orchestra at the same time. I had to make a choice.

My journal entry for 14th January 1972 reads, "Marion is flabbergasted that I am going to drop my flute lessons!!"

On 13th February, aged fourteen, I decided to make music my career. My plan was to teach music, yet I clearly loved performing too.

"The trouble with you is you don't know whether to perform or to teach," Mr Burman observed. In reality, I wanted to do both.

That spring, my brother's music teacher, Michael Beynon, Head of Music at Aylestone School, began giving me some extra music tuition. He told me about a fantastic cellist - Raphael Wallfisch - who lived nearby.

I told him I needed a cello teacher. So Michael Beynon asked the talented, up-and-coming pianist, Marios Papadoupolos, a student at Aylestone School who knew Raphael, if he could help.

After several months, Marios was able to speak to Raphael's mother about me and a meeting was arranged that July. I was sixteen at the time and Raphael was just nineteen.

On 24th July I had my first lesson with Raphael. My journal entry reads "We went upstairs to his room – music study cum bedroom. His cello seems to take up the whole of his bed!"

"Do you like the cello?"

There was only one answer I could give to his question, as Raphael's smiling bright eyes looked hopefully towards me:

I had my tongue in my cheek when I replied "Yes" as I really did not like the cello and was not serious about learning the instrument at all. Clearly I was a good actress, as Raphael agreed to teach me and I became the first of his many students from all over the world.

At this time Raphael was a student at the Royal Academy of Music. He used to tell me that his earnings from giving me cello lessons enabled him to buy some tickets to take his girlfriend (later to become his wife) to the theatre.

Very quickly, I fell in love with the cello - soon my very own, a new Rosetti cello - and so the practising began in earnest. In fact my determination to make up for lost time with my practice increased dramatically.

My brother Bernard did not appreciate my early morning practice sessions while he was studying for school exams. He would bang on the floor in a vain attempt to stop me practising.

He once complained to Michael Beynon: "Can't you stop her practising?" However, by this time I was truly *unstoppable.*

Going to each lesson, one of Raphael's parents would greet me at the door of their home in Willesden. It was either the smiling, well-known pianist Peter Wallfisch, or more often with the few quiet words of his mother, also a cellist, Anita Lasker-Wallfisch. She later wrote about her experiences as a member of the Women's Orchestra in Auschwitz in *Inherit the Truth.*

My orchestral career began in October 1972 when I started playing the cello in the Jewish Youth Orchestra (JYO) under the baton of the charismatic Sydney Fixman.

He was very kind and encouraging, as each week I was able to play a few more notes, continually adding some more "hard bits" and improving my technique on the cello. Again, I had found another musical mentor who I respected and admired.

"What a fantastic and so professional conductor he is," I wrote of him.

Sydney Fixman, through his great storytelling, would inspire us to practise: Quoting from my journal: " '99% hard work 1% talent – all big people, I know the way they work – sheer slog. Practising is a habit and will become part of a routine like getting up the morning.' The way he was talking really made me feel I am doing the right thing and giving myself the chance of success."

My journal entry for 19th November 1972 describes how my viola-playing friend and I coped with our nerves for our first JYO concert at the London Coliseum: *"She was feeling like me, only worse; so sick and butterflying!"*

Whether in a group or as a soloist, even if I was shaking like a leaf before, when it came to the performance I enjoyed every moment of my playing; I knew I wanted to make it my life.

My dedication to achieve this was tracked in practising calendars and in my journals, where I once recorded that I "practised from 8am until 1pm and only stopped once to yawn!"

These valuable and enjoyable performing experiences would make me increasingly determined to become a professional musician who could help others.

Raphael Wallfisch had helped me to get more sound out of the cello than I could ever have imagined. I wrote of my last lesson with him: "I played some of the Vivaldi Sonata, confidently and with large bows, as requested. He made a remark, casual as it was, that perhaps I ought to value: 'There are too many people in the world playing only half: half tone or half confidence.' "

In July 1973 when Raphael went to study at the Julliard School in the USA, the search was on for my next cello teacher. Eva recommended me to Miss Ursula Hess, whose husband, Leslie Hillman, obtained a beautiful Mittenwald cello for me. This wonderful instrument, with its "divine sound" further enhanced my love for the cello.

Of course, with Eva Bernathova teaching me the piano, it was natural for me to want to continue my lessons with her when I went to Music College. So putting 'all my eggs in one basket', Trinity College of Music in London was the only place that I applied for, securing a place to study there in September 1974.

Michael Beynon was now Head of Music at Southgate School and I was now faced with a new kind of opportunity he gave me: start Music College the same day as everyone else, or start a few days late and take what I saw as a once-in-a-lifetime chance to assist with a party of Southgate School children on an educational music cruise.

By deciding to go on the cruise, I was to experience two remarkable highlights of my orchestral life so far.

After a good night's sleep on SS *Uganda*, seasickness caught up with me on my way to an orchestral rehearsal on the upper deck. Along the corridor I happened to meet Hugh Maguire, who was part of the cruise with his Allegri String Quartet. Friendly as he was, I felt so bad that I could hardly talk to him at that moment.

We were rehearsing Don Gillis's *Symphony no. 5 ½, 'A Symphony for Fun'*. As we ploughed through the rough seas of the notorious Bay of Biscay, at one moment there was just the sea as I looked out of the porthole, the next there was the grey sky!

Quoting from my journal: "Playing the cello took my mind off Biscay. Many others were absent due to this. I was happy when they told me that Biscay was the worst part of our voyage. I felt so secure sitting with my cello, watching people toppling over as the ship was rocking."

The other highlight was water slowly dripping down my neck from one of the stalactites, as we played Schumann's "Rhenish" Symphony in the awe-inspiring St Michael's Cave, Gibraltar.

As much as I loved performing, the time was coming for me to share my love of music in another way. Recalling my Grandmother's advice, here was another door of opportunity that I decided to open.

15

Chapter 3
'Failing' my way to success
1974-1978

On Wednesday 16th October 1974 I began teaching music professionally, as I took up Mike Beynon's offer to become the cello teacher at Southgate School where he was now the Head of Music. On the same day I also took up the opportunity he gave me to teach the piano to groups of adults at an evening class, at Moss Hall School, Finchley.

From here my career as a peripatetic cello teacher and a piano teacher seemed set.

"Inspired by the middle-aged beginners at Moss Hall, my mother wanted me to teach her the piano as well. I didn't want to waste my time, but she felt that if middle-aged people at Moss Hall could learn why couldn't she and if she didn't she felt she was wasting the advantage of having me at home. So I gave her half an hour of my time. She seemed quite 'quick' compared to some of my Moss Hall people and her hand didn't go all over the place like some." J (J for Journal) So her lessons with me began and continued intermittently for many years.[1]

Just as my music-teaching career was taking off, something was to happen that was to have a dramatic effect on my life and would be a further influence on my future career path.

"Arriving for my weekly cello lesson at College on Tuesday morning 15th October I caught a fright when Trinity staff told me that my cello teacher Miss Maryse Chomé had strained the wrist of her right hand and they were unsure if she could teach me." J

This had happened to her before and she could not play for six weeks. Fortunately, she *was* able to teach me and I noted how lucky it was that she could still do this. She had the all-important 'other string to her bow'.

---

[1] Josie continued her piano lessons with the author until she passed away, aged ninety-six.

Strangely, that very same evening,

"After three quarters of an hour fantastic cello practice, I nearly busted my left hand after too many double stops. I was SO upset I had to stop practising, I was enjoying myself SO much!!" J

The culmination of my own Repetitive Strain Injury (RSI) really came from over-enthusiasm to practise whilst having poor posture. My doctor told me shortly afterwards that it was a strain and the only cure was as much rest as possible. "If it's that desperate, there is heat treatment", he said and added that I "shouldn't drive".

The pain, from what was described to me as an *'inflamed ligament'*, began near my wrist. It then moved into the thenar muscles, along the side of the thumb of my left hand. It was *"in a dangerous place"* I was told. Later I would also experience the pain in my right hand in a similar place.

The pain would come and go and its cause was often confusing. Did it hurt because I had driven or picked up a shuttlecock the night before?

"I was warned, 'You'll have a permanent weakness.' - but I have chosen not to believe this -'Do not touch your instruments if you are in pain. Be careful or you will not be able to play for weeks.' " J

Even though I was pleading with myself to relax and not be a hypochondriac - I had not yet learned self-hypnosis. Still, sometimes I was terrified of practising. I didn't know if I would be able to play or suddenly have to stop.

Maryse Chomé's similar injury prevented her from playing the cello in the English National Opera Orchestra. It also stopped me from properly progressing with my piano and cello studies as well as performing. As I wrote in my journal:

"I have more or less wasted my first term of Music College".

Miss Chomé could not play the cello and neither could I - it was a bizarre situation. What could we do? We shared our RSI experiences, while she wrote bowing and fingering into the Bach cello suites and other great works in the cello repertoire for me. Having to cancel many piano lessons and having 'cello lessons' without a cello for such a length of time, was very frustrating.

There was no other help or suggestions by Trinity College of Music at this time on how to manage my RSI.

Recalling how my grandmother benefited greatly from using natural approaches to treat things in her life, I began to look into a whole range of complementary treatments. This included having some Alexander Technique lessons[2] - with the now legendary Jean Gibson.

Jean Gibson tried to teach me how to relax and control my muscles and explained that my hand injury was caused by me tensing my arm and wrist. Sadly, these lessons did nothing to help.

In November 1974 I sought treatment from John Sugarman, an osteopath, naturopath and homeopath. He was a great help, as he was to my grandmother and in time, many of our family and close friends.

With backache, neck discomfort and pain in my left hand I arrived at Mr Sugarman feeling like an "old woman".

"If this is something that comes with the profession - I want to get out - I think I am in the wrong line!" J

Apart from my own piano and cello playing being interrupted, tuning the cellos of my students at Southgate School was strenuous and by then I could not even drive a car to get to work.

My musical career could have ended at this point.

Once again, I was unstoppable.

For example, on the piano sometimes I would become the one-handed pianist and just practise for hours with the pain-free hand. By the end of November, although only a very small number of people knew it, I was the "one-handed cellist" in the recording Southgate School made of their production of Benjamin Britten's *Noye's Fludde*.

"Plucking my cello strings and in the absence of vibrato, not making a very nice sound at all, was all very frustrating. I felt such a twit." J

Recovering from RSI took longer than I envisaged. In fact it would affect me on and off for some years. There were days when I could not even write with either hand. With one particular conductor of an orchestras I played in, through his efforts for us to produce the best performances, I would become so tense that it made my hands hurt. This caused "a lot of worry" and what I called 'hand depression'. It was a very difficult time in my life. Many people supported and saw me though this time.

---

[2] Now the Alexander Technique is offered to Music College students. See Chapter 27 where my nail-biting musician client, trained in Alexander Technique, explains how he found TFT tapping more effective.

On 13th January 1975 I had to cancel yet another piano lesson. "Eva said not to be upset. As she spoke to Mum on the phone she could hear sobbing from the staircase. I was in floods by the end of the phone call. I really would rather commit suicide than go through those months again!" Actually, it's not quite true. As I always say - however bad life is, it's still better to be alive than not." J

The worst was still to come.

"Mum told me that Eva suggests I leave cello altogether for three months. As she told me this unbearable thought, my face went scarlet. I could hardly breathe - sob sob! I couldn't even produce tears for such a thing.

Now do I realise just how much the cello means to me – its means a musical life - the thought of only the piano and letting my beautiful cello sit un-played in its case - no orchestra, no chamber music or cello teaching - no LIFE!

But really I suppose this would be the only way not to damage my piano playing too much with it. These past few months have been my worst ever - I can't believe how difficult life suddenly became.

I can't think of anything more harmful that could have happened to me this year. I was not crying alone – Mum was too! She was wholeheartedly devoted to my career and gradually my Dad had become more involved too." J

By the time Mr Sugarman had finished treating me, 'the verdict' was, as he told me, that I had just *'overextended'* my hand and that from now on I could practise! In fact he thought that I should keep playing the cello and therefore keep in practice.

Somehow through these difficult times I found ways to keep myself happy, going out a lot and keeping going with whatever musical activities I could. At least I was able to sing in the Trinity College of Music choir, enjoying performances of the Brahms *German Requiem* and the Bach *St Matthew Passion* in Southwark Cathedral.

As I write this, I realise how much the techniques I would discover in the future could have helped me with the physical and emotional pain.³

By May 1975 I resumed my orchestral playing. I was now the two-handed cellist in Southgate School's performance of the Fauré

---

³ See Chapter 21 with author's more recent RSI experience.

Requiem. "No words can describe my pleasure at being able to do a vibrato and play my cello well for this performance to make up for Noye's Fludde." J

Soon after this, I discussed the wonderful book I was reading at the time with Mr Sugarman. It was called 'I CAN! the key to life's golden secrets' by Ben Sweetland. My interest in psychology was growing and it marked the first of the many personal development books that I have read.

What an impact those two words and the yellow book 'I CAN!' had upon me. They formed a special place in my mind and underpin the message of this book.[4]

Even with all these setbacks, my cello playing still progressed to the extent that, by December, I celebrated being able to take and pass my Grade 8 cello. Prior to my exam I was only worried about my hands and whether they would bother me.

As I warmed up "The examiner could have been in the room and I'd have felt no different. Emotionally I felt on top of everything and able to play my best. In the actual exam Aunty Helena accompanied me most beautifully and Mum turned the pages of her music. I think it was quite something that Mum was not only able to be present in the last grade exam I thought I'd ever do, but also be a part in helping it go smoothly.[5]

I put everything I had into the music and really felt it deeply. I was so proud of my cello. My role model for this was a brilliant child prodigy - my friend Marius May. I tried to look professional and imagined I was playing to an audience in the Wigmore Hall." J

The importance of musical networking and how we come to learn certain instruments is something I have already highlighted in this book. Now it was my turn, as Mike Beynon recommended *me* as a cello teacher to Alex Albani, a 25-year-old French teacher at Aylestone School.

Alex became my first proper private student. I told her my terms were "£1 an hour". Now it was my kind and chatty mother greeting *my* student at the door.

Being Grade 6 piano standard, Alex was more advanced than any of the students I had taught so far. The challenge of teaching her met

---

[4] See Chapter 8 for the 'I can' music lesson.

[5] See Chapter 22, author's Grade 8 flute exam, aged fifty-nine.

once again with the challenge of tuning her cello, an Aylestone school instrument lent to her by Mike. Her first lesson on that Tuesday afternoon, in May 1975, featured her 'A' string breaking!

Recently Alex wrote to me about what it was like for her to take up another musical instrument as an adult:

"It was great having you as a cello teacher as you put no pressure on me; I know I was a little self-conscious to begin with as I was an adult and thought that to learn a musical instrument it was best to start young. If it wasn't for Mike Beynon who lent me my first 'cello and introduced me to you, I would never have learned how to play. Your encouragement and gentle but positive approach soon made me feel at ease and I was amazed at how quickly I was able to succeed in gaining a pleasant sound from this instrument, contrary to my memories of playing the violin at age 11."[6]

When Alex got married in 1978 her husband, author Kevin Desmond, gave her a wedding present of a cello. Through Alex I got to know Kevin. Following him editing my grandmother's book[7] he has also assisted me with the editing of this book.

It was at a Southgate school concert in May 1977 that I had yet another interesting performance experience when I played the first movement of the Elgar cello concerto.

"At the end of the second page I fell into a memory trap - I quickly tried to recover and played a messy bar before I found my place – but by this time I'd scared Mike, my accompanist and he'd stopped, unsure where I'd gone to. But I was sure, so I just carried on and did not blink any eyelid. Over seven bars later he found me.

After the concert he said he hadn't known what to do at the time. Because I didn't make my mistake visually noticeable, the audience were not aware of what had happened." J

As Dame Fanny Waterman once said 'whatever slips may occur, these must be covered up; the show must go on!'[8] Still, I felt ashamed of what had happened. Sadly I did not take up the offer to listen to a good recording of my performance, to hear exactly how I had 'improvised', as I couldn't bear to listen to it at the time. I was

---

[6] Email sent to the author on 23rd July 2014.

[7] 'An Open Mind' The autobiography of Bessie Marks (née Meek) 1989.
See Chapter 33 From typing to tapping.

[8] On Teaching Piano and Performing by Fanny Waterman. First published in 1983 by Faber Music Ltd.

very pleased and amused when I found out, some days later, that several people came up to Mike after the concert and said, "I didn't know there was a cadenza in the first movement of the Elgar cello concerto."

On graduating from Trinity College of Music in 1977, aged 21, I was advised to do a postgraduate certificate in education PGCE - a Music Teachers Certificate (MTC) - giving me the opportunity to obtain a degree. This would involve a further year of study to get the all-important 'bit of paper' - just in case I ever wanted to teach class music in a school, which I had no intention of doing. I did my MTC at the London University, Institute of Education in Bedford Way.

An essential part of this course was the Teaching Practice (TP). Unfortunately any attempts for me to do this at the Jewish Free School (JFS) did not come about, even though Dave Burman thought that it would have been good for both of us.

Following my Teaching Practice at both a local private school, South Hampstead and Kingsbury High School in North West London, a significant meeting with my university tutor John White began:

JW: "What kind of school do you want to teach in?"

R: "None" was my real answer and one that he attempted to draw out of me.

JW: "To be a music teacher you need to have relations with staff and students to arrange things."

At the schools where he saw me do my Teaching Practice, I tended to hide myself and he thought I could not communicate with children.

JW: "Both schools said you would be unhappy in this profession. It is too much effort and could be destroying. You can use yourself better. I don't think you'll cope, you're not 'ready'. You're not assertive enough to be a music teacher."

At the end he told me that he would not award me the Music Teachers Certificate (MTC) as I would fail the Teaching Practice and the only chance was for me to do a further six weeks Teaching Practice in the autumn.

R: "I'm not going to do that!"

I could see his set opinions. It seemed I had done the wrong course. I should have done the peripatetic one, as that was where my

22

real interest lay. So now I would not have my 'bit of paper' and my scope for peripatetic jobs could be limited.

"I cried all the way home. I let it all out to Mum. It was an emotional conversation as really I agreed with John White." J

My lack of interest in class teaching was all too apparent. What chance did I have of winning over John White? It was so difficult to convince him of my capability of teaching classes. Plans were in process for me to take over from Miss Davies, teaching cello at JFS. John White thought that this could be a "happy little thing" for me.

"Once I received it in writing that I had failed my TP, I realised that it was my first important (academic) exam failure. I thought there was not much I could do about it. Stuff their 'bit of paper', but I'm afraid it reflects them turning away a dedicated musician!" J

Yet somehow, being told I did not have what it took to succeed was to ignite yet more determination in me. The musical journey from here is how I 'failed' my way to success!

At first I thought I would make my own way without the MTC. Then as time went on, I thought, 'Why should they get the better of me?' I knew I had to change my attitude before I would attempt the Teaching Practice again. Mr Singer gave me good advice to seek out and ensure that whatever went wrong to cause me to fail did not happen again.

Still, I never thought for one moment I would ever need to use this infamous 'bit of paper'.

Whilst I was considering not completing the course, I had a lot of support. Mr Singer called them "The idiots of the institute!" He thought it was just a bit "not fair" that I did not realise what I was being judged upon: lack of experience.

Friends and family suggested I shouldn't give up and should finish the course, even if it meant retaking the TP with peripatetic teaching.

That was except my grandmother, who was once a gymnastics and dance teacher. She had a very calm reaction to my news: 'Teaching is very hard anyway; you become a nervous wreck. You could do well in private teaching.'

Added to my opinion that I was going down the wrong career path, I was hurting from a difficult personal relationship. It was no wonder that, having failed my teaching practice, I did not really care whether I obtained my MTC or not.

At least I was given the opportunity to sit the written exam. I passed this, despite suffering from the negative opinion of my university tutor; what a terribly dangerous effect such opinions can have.

I wondered which school I would be given to do my TP retake, as I thought it couldn't be better than the ones I had previously, so obviously I was worried! And how would I get the time off to continue to teach cello at Southgate? Once I found out that it was arranged for a school in Paddington, I was miserable about doing my TP again.

When Mike Beynon heard what had happened, he thought if John White 'wasn't doing his job properly', I should have told him so! Mike thought I was quiet and not shy.

The TP retake was hanging over me like a cloud.

However, in this cloud there was a silver lining.

Chapter 4
Miserable to motivated
1978-1983

Fortunately, Mike Beynon, who knew John White very well and was on good terms with him, encouraged me to retake my Teaching Practice (TP) at Southgate School, Enfield. After a few weeks struggle with the Institute, this was rearranged. At last I was now positively motivated as I was already teaching cello at the school. This 'Southgate silver lining' gave me the opportunity to pass my TP, something I had now become very determined to do.

On the last day of my Teaching Practice, John White was very reassuring and led me to believe I would get a positive result this time. "I really can't absorb the fact that from now I am 'beginning my life' and I can choose to earn a living in whatever way I wish." J

On gaining my degree, I was able to increase my peripatetic teaching work to full time. Everything seemed to have fallen into place.

However, the stresses and strains had taken their toll. It was after this very uncertain time that I suffered my first real panic attack as my 'barrel overflowed'.[1]

Shortly afterwards, at the end of April 1979 Laurence Wiseman and I were introduced to each other at the engagement party of our respective cousins, as our families knew we both had a love of music and sport.

Then one evening, just a month later, Dave Burman called to ask me whether I would be interested in teaching music as his assistant at JFS. It was "a real opportunity" and an offer I could not refuse - even though in the past I had thought I would never do class teaching! Of course, I was only able to accept because I now had that all-important 'bit of paper' - the Music Teachers Certificate (MTC)!

On my arrival at JFS I was keen to do well. I needed help as there were barriers to get through. "Dave appreciates my conscientiousness and with this I'll get there in the end.

---

[1] Dr Doris Rapp and the *'Barrel Effect'* analogy

I feel right for the job. Well suited to school and kids." J

What a turnaround!

Just after Christmas that year I heard that the distinguished young pianist and prodigy Terence Judd had ended his own life. For those in my family who knew him, it was like mourning a relative. I had come to know Terence some four years previously, through my grandmother introducing me to his mother and me babysitting for his younger sister.

Terence was the first of a few talented musicians, whom I knew very well, that 'did not make it' further into the musical world, or even in life. The impact on me of his suicide only added to my deep desire to help musicians.

Taking advantage of a double bass that was not in use in the JFS music store cupboard, I set about learning yet another musical instrument and one that was *truly* bigger than me! I was warned that the strings would be expensive to replace. Fearing a worse string-breaking experience than I had with my cello, my time playing the double bass was short lived, lasting only as long as my class teaching post at the school.

Apart from being involved helping with the school shows, the highlight of my time teaching at JFS, was assisting with rehearsing the school choir for their historic performance at Hampstead Synagogue for my wedding to Laurence Wiseman. After some traditional songs, *Baruch Haba* and *Hariu*, as it was the first night of the Jewish Festival of Chanukah, they also sang *Ma-oz Tsur*. All of the musical arrangements were by their conductor Dave Burman. Then they gave a beautiful rendition of *Ha-lo tsi vi ti cha*,[2] composed especially for us by Dave Burman, with my cousin Daphne Meek as soloist.

Due to a misunderstanding as to when the choir were to perform their welcome song *Baruch Haba*, a warden would not allow me into the synagogue. I was so annoyed that I could only hear this song from behind a closed door. When he did let me in I stomped up the aisle to the sound of...silence! Neither the JFS and Hampstead Synagogue choirs, nor even the confused organist, were to be heard at this point!

---

[2] Be strong and of good courage thy God is with thee withersoever thou goest. Joshua 1:9

It was only after we had been married for nearly a year, that I discovered Laurence's musical secret. We were at a concert at the Royal Festival Hall, where a clarinet trio was being performed. Suddenly Laurence revealed to me that he had a clarinet under our dining room table! Prior to our marriage it was hidden under his bed in the flat where he used to live. He had not played it since he was at school.

Inspired by the concert and with some typical Rosemary -style encouragement, first thing the next morning Laurence offered to play me his clarinet. After thirteen years of it being untouched, I could not believe he would be able to play *anything* at all. So when I heard the sounds of 'Ode to Joy', a real melody, there was more joy than I could ever have imagined - I was amazed.

Mike recommended him to a clarinet teacher and soon after Laurence and I were able to play together in the Edgware Symphony Orchestra; especially enjoying performances under the baton of the calm and talented conductor Mark Wigglesworth.

The deputy head of JFS, Mrs Wagerman, observed my teaching in October 1982. "She was first person ever to praise my teaching and it meant a lot. She was extremely complimentary... 'The children are very fortunate to have such a skilled musician to teach them.' " J

Still there were small numbers taking up music and she told me that, if I left, they would have to have a 'part-timer' to replace me.

After over three years teaching at JFS and with no promises from the Headmaster that I could become Head of the Department, I accepted the fact that there was "*no scope*" for me at the school. I had become more and more interested in furthering my career and realised I would need to leave in order to achieve this.

It was a stressful time and my 'barrel' was now overflowing in a different way, with physical effects on my stomach!

In February 1983 the Headmaster informed Dave that if I were to leave, all he would get would be a supply teacher next term to assist him.

"Thus begins cut down of music at JFS. So will I leave the 'sinking ship'?" J

I thought the only change was that I would be going to a new school, reducing my hours to working part-time as a class music teacher and allowing time for more music making myself. Yet soon some seeds were about to ripen, with some very new and surprising skills.

Chapter 5
'Rosh Pinah' - the 'cornerstone'
ראש פינה
1983-1998

"Plants, then dogs, then babies," our friend Kevin Desmond had told us. As I was now working part-time we acquired a new addition to our family, our dog Sandy. In time, he joined in by 'singing' with our musical household.

After a short while, unhappy in my new job as a class music teacher at Claremont High School, I happened to attend a JFS reunion. It was here that I was fortunate enough to meet my former colleague Mervyn Leviton, now the Headmaster of Rosh Pinah Primary School, Edgware. He offered me the post of music teacher at his school - an opportunity I could not turn down.

In January 1984, I took over from Audrey Brain, sister-in-law of the British virtuoso French horn player, Dennis Brain. Rather than have me observe her teaching to model her methods, she encouraged me to teach my own way and I certainly followed her advice.

Although I had continued teaching cello at JFS after I resigned as a class teacher there, I now decided to stop my peripatetic teaching and concentrate on building up music at Rosh Pinah. So, with me as cello teacher and employing the services of my friend Judy Gabriel as a violin teacher, instrumental lessons began at Rosh Pinah. That snowy day in January 1985 "Rosh Pinah and Mr Leviton were bubbling in excitement for the start of violin lessons." J

Later I increased the range of instruments offered, adding flute and brass. My husband Laurence also joined our thriving music department, teaching clarinet and saxophone, as well as drums. He was a great communicator with the children and taught very successfully, achieving good results with his students in ABRSM exams.

I found a simple way to encourage a large number of children to learn musical instruments - by demonstration and then allowing them to have hands-on experience of the actual instrument itself.

In my student days at JFS and for some years afterwards, I had attended many concerts with the Royal Philharmonic Orchestra (RPO) at the Royal Festival Hall, as my housemaster, Michael Webber, was chairman of the RPO club. Following in the footsteps of Brian Snary, I was very proud that as well as establishing a school band, it was now *me* who had assembled an orchestra, which of course I called the 'RPO' - Rosh Pinah Orchestra. So here was one other 'instrument' I also played…the 'orchestra'! Perhaps it was the only way I could play all those instruments at the same time, as in my 'one-man band'.

Apart from conducting at Rosh Pinah, I also had an opportunity one evening to conduct part of a rehearsal of the Edgware Symphony Orchestra. I quickly learned what it meant when some of the instrumentalists were missing - confusion for the conductor! However, I enjoyed leading the cello section in a number of amateur orchestras for many years.

It was in 1986, just two years after I began teaching at Rosh Pinah, that my 'parenting' career also began: our son David was born on the 5th of March.

When he was in his cot in his small bedroom, I wanted to play music to him. No, not the harp! - Just something more portable than my piano or cello. One day Laurence spotted a flute in a junk shop nearby our home in Queensbury. This was the beginning of my returning to playing the flute.

Before long, I was offering to perform on this instrument at David's nursery school. It was just an informal performance to his small class. Yet as I began to play, I hyperventilated, going dizzy, after only a few notes.

It was soon after, due to the pain I experienced caused by Bruxism - teeth grinding, and temporomandibular joint (TMJ) problems, that John Sugarman referred me to Anthony Newbury, a private dentist in Harley Street. During my dental treatment Mr Newbury suggested I see a friend of his who could "clear your mind."

This was my introduction, in July 1990, to Dr Brian Roet and indeed to the wonderful world of Ericksonian Self-Hypnosis. During my first session with Dr Roet, a former doctor and Australian footballer, he told me how he had had personal lessons from Dr Milton Erickson. I in turn now had some very powerful experiences using Self-Hypnosis, particularly realising how it could work where medical intervention and medication did not.

For example, one open evening at Rosh Pinah I could not open my mouth to speak to parents. I was suffering from pain in my jaw. My doctor visited me at home yet was unable to help. The following day, hypnosis enabled me to open my mouth once again as the pain disappeared.

Using this most effective treatment for pain relief and helping to overcome my panic attacks with Brian Roet's guidance became like a 'lifesaver' to me. I learned so much from him, especially about the power of the mind.

It was in my seventh year teaching at Rosh Pinah that, unknown to anyone else, I suffered my first real experience of stage fright. Many musicians go through some form of this at some point in their musical career and most keep it a secret if they possibly can.

It occurred during an ordinary school assembly. I was playing a piano arrangement of *Dance of the Knights* from Prokofiev's ballet music for *Romeo and Juliet* when all of a sudden my mind just went blank. I simply could not find the chords, which I had experienced no trouble in playing only moments before.

I thought I knew exactly what had triggered this. With some children in the hall losing their attention, I immediately doubted the quality of my own playing. The professional pianist who had come in to play to us the very same music earlier in the week was excellent. How could I possibly match up to him?

The one benefit of my own stage fright, from which I recovered so well using self-hypnosis, was that it has since given me an insight into the performance anxiety of musicians and public speakers whom I have been able to help since, adopting some important techniques that I learned at this time. For example, while giving me a few lessons, Chani Smith, our flute teacher at Rosh Pinah, became the first person to teach me diaphragmatic or belly breathing. That soon put an end to my hyperventilating on my flute. Yet once again the busier I became with my teaching, the less I would pick up my instrument.

My natural interest in helping people continued to grow. In particular - children's tummy aches. I would teach them diaphragmatic breathing by getting them to lie down on the floor and to place a salad spinning bowl on their tummies. By the way, this spinner was just one of the unusual items I had in the music room which we used for musical sound effects in compositions.

I encouraged the children to keep their chests still and watch the bowl rise as they breathed from their diaphragm. After a few minutes of this, they no longer had any need to visit the medical room. However, for some it took a little longer to learn these breathing techniques.

Once I was visiting a different classroom and a student screamed out in front of everyone "I can do it!" "Do what?" I said. "I can breathe properly now" she replied, delighted that after a few days she had mastered the diaphragmatic breathing I had shown her.

With the support and interest that the Headmaster, Mervyn Leviton, showed in my musical endeavours, I was very successful at Rosh Pinah.

Working alongside staff, most notably my friend Lorna Gordon, and with parental input, I produced and directed many popular musical productions. These included, for example, *Joseph and the Amazing Technicolor Dreamcoat, Oliver, Fiddler on the Roof*; new compositions such as *The Note That Got Away* by Adam Collins,[1] the computer musical *Hackback* or even operas like *The Pirates of Penzance* and *The Mikado*! The many extra hours I spent arranging the band parts were well worthwhile.

Lorna was an amazing drama teacher. She could act any of the parts so well, and to my delight would often demonstrate this to the children. When she saw me knitting in the staff room, something we both loved to do, she would jokingly say, "I get worried when I see you knitting," as she thought things may not be going well with the production.

---

[1] Adam used to accompany ballet classes nearby where I lived. I helped him out by doing some of these accompaniments. He took some involvement with our production of his composition 'The Note That Got Away,' insisting we did the 'finale' when I wondered whether to include it or not. He also played drum-kit in the actual performance. Sadly a short time later he ended he own life. He was the third significant musician I knew who did not make it in the musical world.

However, this was just another of my ways of relaxing. I still have the hat I made with the leftover wool Lorna gave me from the scarf she knitted.

These productions gave me wonderful experience, further preparing me to help performers in the future. They became legendary and something of a phenomenon, with Rosh Pinah students, parents and staff impatiently asking me what the next year's show was, even before the end of the current production.

It got to such a point that, when I was expecting our second child, Natalie and after having being away from school for six weeks suffering with *hyperemesis gravidarum* (severe vomiting in pregnancy), the first question I was asked by the children when I returned to work was: "Are we still going to do Oliver?"

Whenever I meet past students, the question is always asked, "Which show were you in?" rather than "which class were you in?" Even my clarinet, saxophone and drum-kit playing husband Laurence and for some productions, our trumpet-playing son David, took part. It was very special for me to be able to teach music to our own children, who were both students at Rosh Pinah. They certainly benefited from all the musical activities that were on offer.

As you see from the title of this chapter, *Rosh Pinah* means 'cornerstone'. My fourteen very happy years at this school, with the golden years of music making there, were really the cornerstone of my musical career.

I might still have been at the school and this book would not have existed in its present form, if Mervyn Leviton had not left Rosh Pinah, to be replaced by a new Head Teacher. I called the day he resigned a '*black hole day*'. Changes were rapid and I did not get on with the new Head.

A new chapter in my life was about to begin, where out of adversity great things arrive.

Chapter 6
Self-Hypnosis, my pathway
to better music making
1998 – 2000

During this stressful period and time of change, I noticed that I was not performing on the piano as well as usual. Playing some music by Chopin one day, I realised that my fingers were not moving freely around the piano keys. I decided to do something about this when a colleague from Rosh Pinah told me that she was attending some Alexander Technique (AT) lessons. This was my second encounter with AT and once again it did not work for me. There had to be something else and I was close to finding it.

I started to hear and see "unhappy bunnies" - the Rosh Pinah staff - all around me. "Tears, upset, sadness, pressure, headaches! MADNESS, it goes on! Through it all I am looking to the future. It is my sense of humour and that of others that has got me through." J

In my efforts to cheer everyone up, I got the school singing "SMILE", the song composed by Stanley King, the grandfather of one of the students.

I realised I was not getting respect and appreciation from the new head.

I was ready to move on and in my time of need, ready to look at new opportunities. Yet it can be hard to come out of that comfort zone, especially when it is something you love and is your career. And to move on where? And when?

My interest in practical psychology began the day I took my Music Teachers Certificate (MTC) psychology exam. I wrote about a horrible experience I had that morning and believed that was how I passed my theoretical MTC exam.

Then came the way I helped myself through my own difficulties, after becoming fascinated by psychology books. A course in assertiveness I did at this time got me even further involved. At that training I was as much concerned about how others had been helped as I was with my own problems. A few years prior to this I had told

Mr Sugarman I wanted to help others. However, my reflexologist discouraged me from this plan and suggested I did it through my music.

"Who knows, maybe in the end that's what it'll be! I'm like Gran was with her nature cure. When I believe in something then I want to help others." J

I again told Mr Sugarman about my ideas for the future. His message was clear: "Make yourself strong. Empower yourself."

Then, with the shake-up at Rosh Pinah, I had a chat with my friend Michele Ben Moshe. We had been friends since January 1989 when we met while settling our children into their first week at Rosh Pinah nursery and exchanging our experiences of Bruxism, or teeth grinding.

Even though Michele had previously told me of her mother's occupation, it was as if it had never registered properly. Although we had got to know each other at her granddaughter Dalia's birthday parties, we did not discuss her work. At one of those parties, the entertainer was late. Being a teacher and musician. I quickly sorted the children out and became the stand-in entertainer until the real one arrived. "That girl's got magic" her mother told Michele.

Now the right time had arrived for me to take up Michele's suggestion; to speak to her mother, Molly-Ann Smith,[1] who was a concert pianist and piano teacher and who, at a similar age to myself, had become a hypnotherapist. (As there were no courses around, she was taught hypnosis by her piano student; a doctor, who was an anaesthetist, in exchange for piano lessons.) This gave me a dream idea that I was soon to make come true.

It happened on 5th February 1998. I will never forget the look of horror on my mother's face as she heard of my husband Laurence's idea that I apply for the post of Deputy Head of Rosh Pinah! I had to come up with a real alternative career quickly. The very next day I called Molly-Ann from the staff room at school. I knew from her words of encouragement that I had what it takes.

Only now did I find out that Molly-Ann also knew about Dr Brian Roet's remarkable work. She then told me about Stephen Brooks, an excellent and now legendary trainer of Ericksonian Hypnotherapy

---

[1] Molly-Ann Smith was the first piano teacher of pianist Michael Roll, before she passed him on, at the age of six, to Dame Fanny Waterman.

and Indirect Hypnosis; just the same method of hypnosis that I wanted to study. He ran seminars in similar techniques to those I had already been using with Brian Roet. Both had spent time studying with Dr Milton Erickson.

Stephen Brooks's Ericksonian hypnotherapy course was the first of its kind in Europe. By chance there was a free introductory hypnosis evening with him coming up in a few weeks.

"I jumped at it and booked myself in. As I sat in the staff room I smiled that I had got a free place. I was so excited and looking forward to the 27th February." J

Mr Sugarman had suggested other courses to me and whilst those doors had closed to me, this opened.

"I'll regard it as a superb extension to my education. I also hope that in the future I can earn a living through it (not standing in a hair dressers!)" J

Yes, hairdressing was one of my other career 'options', as it is another sideline of mine. Having suffered from varicose veins, my mother had discouraged me from getting my first job as a teenager working in a hairdresser; she knew I would have been standing for long hours. Still, a desire to pursue this occupation, perhaps to do something different with my hands, stayed with me. As soon as it grew long enough, I began to cut our own childrens' hair. Then in 1994 I took a course in hairdressing. The biggest lesson I had here was how to listen to people and how to give people phobias!

One evening I brought along my friend Michele's daughter Dalia, aged 8, as a model. Watched by Michele, I began cutting Dalia's hair carefully and listening to her every suggestion as to how she wanted it. Then as Michele went out of the room for a smoke, the instructor on the course took hold of the scissors and chop chop chop…….. I could see Dalia's distress and although I realised Michele knew it was not my fault, I quickly decided to stick to family and friends haircuts only!

Being such a good friend and not wanting to upset me further or stop me from pursuing a hairdressing career - knowing only nature could grow the hair back and that time only could resolve this problem - Michele did not tell me what really happened after that day. It was only years later that she revealed the full story of Dalia's phobia of having her hair cut, resulting from this trauma. Until she was nineteen and her hair was at waist length, Dalia would only allow her hairdresser to 'seal the ends'.

Still, I would get itchy fingers whenever I saw someone who clearly needed a trim. This led me, at one rehearsal of the Edgware Symphony Orchestra (ESO), to offer a haircut in the break to our conductor Mark Wigglesworth, a student at the Royal Academy of Music at the time. He found some reason to be too busy the next week for me to do this and shortly afterwards appeared with a new haircut!

Brian Roet describes his work as "Challenging restricting beliefs". I certainly had no restricting beliefs that I could help people through hypnosis. Once back at home, on the day I made those all-important phone calls from the staff room, I stood excitedly in our kitchen and asked Laurence if he would support me in my new career. "Yes" was his immediate reply. Then I told him what it was! "Do you really want to have the hassle of other people's problems?" he continued.

In advance of the hypnosis evening, I had my first 'official' client, my father. The only known prior experience I had was the previous year, when I helped our son David over a fear of rain. I realised then that I had potential.

Now in his time of need, my father welcomed my help, as after some nine years of symptoms, he had finally been diagnosed in 1997 with *Progressive Supranuclear Palsy* (PSP); the same disease that the actor, comedian, musician and composer Dudley Moore suffered from. Even the year before my father's diagnosis, I had observed that although he could sing and compose, he could not move his fingers to play C E G, with the 1st, 3rd and 5th fingers of the right hand on the piano. They went 1st to 2nd to 4th. Using my new therapeutic techniques and music, I set about making my father's quality of life as good as it could be under the circumstances. Perhaps then, I could say he was my first music and therapy client.

On the hypnosis evening, I booked myself onto Stephen Brooks's combined diploma course in Hypnotherapy, Cognitive Psychotherapy and NLP Neuro Linguistic Programming. It was my "entry into self-hypnosis" and was one of the easiest decisions of my life. I did this only after I had spoken to someone who had already completed this course; they had spent six months researching the best one available before embarking on it. I knew it was 'win win'. I could use what I would learn for myself, as well as be able to help others.

From now on I became, like Molly-Ann Smith, both a piano teacher and a hypnotherapist.

Whilst I studied with Stephen Brooks in London, Molly-Ann took the same seminar in Birmingham. One weekend for some reason I missed a London seminar weekend, so I travelled to Birmingham to complete it. On that weekend, Molly-Ann introduced me to another delegate, Dr Colin Barron, who I later found out was a past medical student of the father of my friend Judy, to whom this book is dedicated. Colin, who by chance was staying in the same hotel as me, kindly offered to carry my bags to the seminar the next day. Little did I realise how in the years to come he would help me with far more than my bags.

Back at school I welcomed the session the staff were given one day on stress management. Afterwards, I started to use the relaxation script on my mother and also made a recording for her. From her positive feedback, I realised I had found my "hypnotic voice".

"I want to achieve success in helping people – I was so keen to help Mum and Dad and want this to give me confidence with others." J

I was fortunate my parents had open minds and that I could help them.

I learned much from this experience.

By now the situation at the school had worsened. It was a time of incredible change. I could see I would be losing my 'working' family. As with all changes, only later does one see why and how things happen.

As I collected our daughter Natalie from the school playground, other concerned parents often asked me: "What are you going to do?" I told them I was going to be a hypnotherapist, although at the time it was still a dream.

Holding onto my dream, and training with Stephen Brooks, actually helped me to come away from Rosh Pinah in a far better condition than did many of my other colleagues who left the school later on.

"The Course helped me cope with changes at Rosh Pinah. I enjoy the studying immensely. It is interesting and calming." J

The new head was the catalyst for sending me on my way to help so many others and myself.

Right now it was time for a new identity. I was once again looking at new ways to expand my musical career.

With the sudden arrival of extra free time, I wrote down a list of things I wanted to do. Somewhere on that list was music therapy and book writing. "I've wanted to be a writer since about nine or ten years old. Now my dream could be a little closer." J

Despite being advised not to give up my day job, I next planned to become a music examiner. Such an occupation can change someone's life. Yet this was not to be, as the application I made was turned down. Apparently, as I was told, ABRSM were not looking for additional examiners at that time. Although I might have regretted this as being in the wrong place at the wrong time, this was to prove a turning point, which would take my life in a very different direction.

Now free from a regular teaching post, I was able to take on a lot of work doing piano accompanying. Once again, I found myself entertaining in residential homes and day care centres. This gave me a valuable opportunity to observe first-hand the beneficial effect music can have on people.

Through it, I was able to put to good use my abilities to sing and perform on the piano, cello, flute, recorders, accordion and the guitar. I sometimes felt that these instruments were like people, almost as if they were competing for the chance to be played! Of course, it was really just myself wanting, as ever, to be the 'one-man band'.

Once again, looking for a more portable instrument, I had started playing the accordion for a very special reason. I had always wanted to learn this instrument after missing the chance to purchase an accordion I had spotted in a jumble sale when I was at primary school.

As for my own piano playing, I began to notice how much more easily my fingers were moving around the keys. I knew it was my new life with hypnosis that was behind this.

My more flexible timetable also allowed me to take on some supply teaching. I worked for a short while at some special schools, Mapledown and Whittlesea, where there were some children with autism. I naturally used musical percussion instruments to help communicate with them. I attended a Music Therapy workshop given by Harrow Music Service at this time, which I found very interesting.

Meanwhile, my family began to notice I was talking in a different way when I was speaking to my private music students' parents. "Stop doing your 'hypno stuff' " they would say. However by this time, once again, I was unstoppable. This was to be the beginning of where music and therapy would really come together for me.

The course with Stephen Brooks was a very practical one. Because I had already been using self-hypnosis for some eight years, the techniques came very naturally to me. I quickly realised I was becoming an effective hypnotherapist.

This feeling was reinforced in the early stages of the course when I helped a delegate who was having sleeping problems. After just a few minutes sitting in an ordinary upright chair, they commented, "it was the best night's sleep I have had in years."

I have since found this experience very useful in helping others with sleeping or energy problems; it has also very useful for me. Yes, teaching music is very entrancing and it could be easy to fall asleep during a lesson if you are overtired or affected by fragrances. If I have ever been short of sleep, I learned from helping this delegate on the course how quickly one could refresh oneself using self-hypnosis.

As a child I had not been keen to practise the piano for my teacher Miss Zareen and my mother had to give me various incentives to do so. Then at Music College, with my long hours of practising and studying music, including four hours of piano and two hours of cello, my mother used to help me get through it by chatting and eating chocolate. The outcome of this was that I became a chocoholic!

On the hypnotherapy course, to some extent I was able to overcome this addiction. However I did still have cravings. Later on I will tell you how I finally beat this addiction.

In 1999 I obtained my Diploma as a qualified practitioner in Ericksonian Hypnosis, Psychotherapy and NLP Neuro Linguistic Programming. I proudly kept the £20 note I received from my first client - a family member - in a frame for quite some time.

Although NLP was included in the Hypnotherapy course, I wanted to study more from the masters. So in March 2000 I did a further training in NLP with Paul McKenna, Dr Richard Bandler and Michael Breen. Dr Colin Barron was by chance on the same course and in one of the breaks he told me about a new therapeutic technique he was now using.

I was soon to discover what this remarkable new approach was to helping people. Now I was really about to use my hands for something very different and it was not hairdressing!

Chapter 7
My discovery of TFT
Into the 21ˢᵗ century

In September 1999 I found my way back to class teaching in schools for just a few hours a week. It happened only because my friend and colleague Susan Moss - the lady who actually became the deputy head of Rosh Pinah - offered me a music specialist and cello teaching position at Barnfield Primary School where she was now the head teacher.

Once again I had a 'real job'. It helped to give me a focus and of course, a regular income. Most of all, I had a very special relationship with the children and it gave me the opportunity to put into practice my musical ideas and experience. Although I was sorry to leave when, in time, they did not need my services any more, I was happy that at least now there were plans in place for the musical life of the school to continue. *"Now it remains to be seen how I will fill this gap. Will I ever go back into a music teaching job such as this again? I feel determined to fill the space well."* J
"TEXTBOOK FOR BETTER LIVING"
(The opening title of my 2000 journal.)

My only regular music class teaching job now was at Stag Lane First School, for just two hours of work a week. I thought the OFTSTED inspector's report: *"30 smiling faces"* would be a good note on which to leave and end my class-teaching career.

Around these musical goings on, something very significant in my life happened. The last time I phoned my friend Judy Gabriel was on her birthday in the year 2000. As she reflected on her life, she told me she felt her biggest achievement was bringing up her three children, who by now were teenagers. Sadly from there things went rapidly downhill, as she was told she could not be cured from cancer, which she had bravely fought for some years. A few months later, on 24ᵗʰ June, Judy passed away (see Chapter 35).

"I have known Judy since we were fourteen and it was like we went through everything together. She was my old school friend, but my most special one due to our music and similarities.

My grief has been soaked up by my concern for the loved ones she left behind. Judy has been a part of my family to me and her family were like part of mine.

My best way of expressing my emotions was in *Liebestraum, Nocturne no.3* by Liszt. It sums up the love, hurt, anger, joy and fun of all of Judy's life and death. It was wonderful how my own piano playing could make me cry!!" J

In many ways Judy and I were alike, yet we could be very different as well. Something bound us together and I believe this was our vulnerability. We had our music in common, although very different methods. Through my recent work in hypnosis we had become closer, discussing Judy's interest in the philosophies of Suzuki, an internationally known method of teaching music.

Now I realised that all those things that Judy talked to me of would no longer be shared; for example, how she combined Suzuki teaching with her own methods. It was this very thought that gave me the idea to write a book on my own music teaching methods. Deciding I would dedicate it to Judy, I set out to achieve my dream and started keeping notes on my music teaching in little notebooks. I called these 'Music All The Way'. Although I did not know it at the time, these notes were soon to change dramatically when I acquired some remarkable and effective new skills. Skills that would change the way I taught music forever.

I have a vague, yet distinct memory, of the day I briefly saw a man on television demonstrating and talking about a finger - tapping technique. At the time it meant very little to me and I admit I took little notice of this programme.

Then one spring day in 2001, I was chatting with my friend Michele Ben Moshe, when she told me that her mother, Molly-Ann Smith, was now using something called Thought Field Therapy (TFT). "Why don't you do what my mum is doing? Speak to her." Hadn't I once heard Michele say this to me before?

Dr Colin Barron had told Molly-Ann that she was being unfair to her clients by not using TFT with them. She had now trained as a TFT practitioner and was successfully using this new technique with her clients.

My father's factory had manufactured bedroom furniture.[1] He used to teach our family to tell everyone that they had 'the finest sliding doors in the country', which I am sure they were. As I was about to decide whether I would pursue these new TFT techniques, one might say this was my very own 'sliding door moment'.

Ever since qualifying as a hypnotherapist, I had been running a peer support group at my home. At one of these meetings, a colleague who had also done some of the teaching on the Stephen Brooks hypnotherapy course, introduced us to a tapping technique called EFT, or Emotional Freedom Techniques. Gary Craig had developed EFT. He was a former student of Dr Roger Callahan - the founder of TFT (see Chapter 34).

The tapping protocols and affirmations of EFT interested me. I tried them on some family and friends. Although it did not help them much, I was curious. I wanted to see if it could help me with a personal issue: my addiction to chocolate. Let me explain. During this period, every day I used to share a 'healthy' cottage cheese salad at lunchtime with my husband Laurence. However, I would frequently choke during and after our meal. Then as soon as Laurence went out of the kitchen, I would search for something sweet to overcome my cravings. The only way I could avoid eating chocolate was not to have any in our house.

Although I worked through a book about "Emotional Eating" with EFT procedures, I did not obtain any real benefit from it. However, like many who experience some positive effects of EFT, I knew I was onto something good. I just wanted it to work better.

When Michele again mentioned to me how well the TFT was going with her mother, I decided to see if I too could benefit from this technique before using it with my clients. I arranged to train as a TFT practitioner myself, with Jo Cooper, who had also taught Molly-Ann. I was fortunate that Jo was running a weekend course in Muswell Hill, North London, just twenty minutes away from my home.

Over the years I have found that people have discovered TFT in different ways: by reading the self – help book, *Tapping the Healer Within* by Dr Roger Callahan with Richard Trubo, or through

---

[1] *'The Finest Sliding Doors in the Country' The Story of M Woolf furniture & the Woolf Family, 2017*

consulting a practitioner, or seeing it demonstrated in public on television or YouTube, or quite simply by being told about it in some form. Mine was a very first-hand - or first-fingers - introduction, very practical and personal.

15th July 2001: "So here comes the next life changer - this weekend I did a course on TFT all for £350. It would involve me teaching self - help techniques and is an art form. Going through my Thought Fields last night didn't allow me much sleep. I'm so excited!" J

Firstly, Jo told us about Dr Roger Callahan of La Quinta, California, who had been developing TFT since 1979 and shared her opinion that he was a genius. She revealed to us that Roger had kept detailed notes on what he was developing for over 20 years. Ian Graham brought over TFT to the UK in November 1996 and so it was still very much in its infancy.

Four of us were on the course. Before taking us through the tapping techniques, Jo invited each of us to think of something that we were a little afraid of, or anxious about. Worms came into my mind. In 1982 I had experienced a trauma while gardening when I saw a worm split in two - both halves then wriggled their separate ways back into the earth. Consequently, gardening and walking in the park or along the street on warm wet days, became difficult.

Following Jo's instructions, we tapped several sequences of acupressure points with our fingers - no verbal affirmations were needed, unlike with EFT – and soon each of us had eliminated our problems. I was so busy tapping that I was unable to observe the benefit the others in the group were getting; something I was very keen to do. Little did I realise how many people I was to observe getting help from TFT in future years.

As a result of my tapping, I could not access my previous problem. It was a drifting, blurred feeling and I now could not picture it at all.

I am so glad that I had this reaction, as it has enabled me to identify with others. So many times since then, I have heard similar responses to tapping a TFT sequence when helping others.

Even now, as I watch my fearless one-year-old great nephew Jack attempt to grab a worm, which manages to escape into the grass - or when I am gardening or walking on damp days and meet my friends, the worms, I am grateful that those few minutes of a TFT tapping treatment have remained effective.

"The war in Kosovo is over." J 12.6.99

Jo told us of her experiences using TFT for trauma in Kosovo. At the time I could not grasp the true significance of this and how it would affect my own interest in helping people suffering from post-traumatic stress disorder (PTSD) in the future. However, there was something that Jo told us that I was very passionate about.

A year after our faithful old dog, Sandy, was put down, we had recently acquired a needy little rescue dog called Candy. What excited me the most in my TFT training was the work that Jo was doing with TFT and animals, such as horses and dogs. Candy was clearly waiting in the wings for TFT!

There was more drama to come on my TFT Algorithm training course. We were asked to focus on an anxious thought so we could measure our Heart Rate Variability (HRV). Having a great imagination, I was rather too good at this and gave myself a panic attack! A kind word from another delegate calmed me down before I had a chance to use TFT on that occasion. Oh, if only I could have told Jo, I am sure she would have had an effective tapping sequence for me.

Then through doing a TFT Voice Technology (VT) test for Individual Energy Toxins (IETS), I discovered I was sensitive to a number of foods. Even with some symptoms of Irritable Bowel Syndrome (IBS), I reacted - as some of my clients were to do in the future - by saying to myself: "I couldn't possibly change my diet."

Only later was I to discover the link between Irritable Bowel Syndrome (IBS) and anxiety.

In the weeks to come, whenever the lunchtime choking continued after my 'healthy' salad, I decided to take those sensitivity tests seriously - another positive turning point in my life.

After my own first and powerful experiences of TFT, I was very curious and keen to share it with others and observe its effects. First in line was…my dog!

Tapping with people and pets - little did I know just how much my weekend with Jo was to change my life and those of the many with whom I have since shared TFT.

I quickly found TFT to be much more speedy and effective than EFT, so from then on, I had no reason to return to it, other than to learn how to use it to help people with many emotional and physical issues.

As part of our TFT practitioner course, we had to do some case studies. Molly-Ann Smith suggested I submit an extra one about our dog Candy.

At this time it was unusual for NLP practitioners or Hypnotherapists to use tapping techniques as they were not yet well-known. I was one of the first to do so and with my background in music, it was inevitable that I would soon find a way to incorporate TFT here as well.

I was now doing a lot of piano accompanying, which was to give me further valuable opportunities. With my new therapeutic skills, I found I was able to help musicians really perform at their best, unlike the first time I ever accompanied someone for a music exam (See Chapter 20).

I was not looking for another music teacher post. However, one day in 2001 my husband Laurence came across a newspaper advert for a music teacher at Buxlow Preparatory School. When I visited the Head teacher, Barbara Lancaster, I could not resist the opportunity to accept the post at this unique school.

"Once again, I have found a Head Teacher who is giving me every encouragement in my musical endeavours at the only private school I have worked in. I have even taught a few music lessons with my dog Candy on my lap or next to me, to help some of the children get over their fear of dogs. It has been a joyous time having two afternoons 'off' each week to go and have some fun at Buxlow." J

When the well-known Hypnotherapist Paul Mckenna began using TFT and including it in his best-selling books, he said it should be "shouted from the rooftops and taught in schools." It was at Buxlow School that I personally had my first opportunity to do just this.

I showed the students how tapping the PR spot (the side of the hand) can be useful when learning anything new. Where better to use it than when teaching the recorder, a deceptively difficult, yet popular first instrument for so many children. Now with TFT, I had another 'string to my bow', as I could help children with performance anxiety.

In 2002 I took to the stage myself in a new way. Since my school days I had come to love opera, and I would regularly attend the performances of my cousin Daphne Meek in the Brent Opera.

When at Rosh Pinah, I had taken just a few singing lessons with Daphne. Little did she know I used to practise singing while cycling to school. In 2002 I joined the chorus of the Brent Opera, singing soprano in *The Merry Wives of Windsor* and later *La Cenerentola* (*Cinderalla*) at St Andrew's Church in West Hampstead. When I started, it was very close to the performance and I did not know if I would have time to learn the part, so the musical director offered me the chance of singing back-stage. This was not for me! I was far more interested in the drama on stage itself. It was a very enjoyable and valuable experience that proved to be useful with the vocal coaching work I came to do. I also saw just how much work goes on behind the scenes to produce an opera. I also later discovered through TFT, that I was sensitive to the stage make up - another example of my 'barrel overflowing'.[2]

In June 2004, I was fortunate enough to continue my diagnostic training in TFT in London with Dr Roger Callahan himself, who had come over from California. This was the first time I had met Roger and his wife Joanne Callahan. I learned much when I observed Roger simply remove his jacket to 'treat' himself when something was 'zapping' his speech. He was also suffering from a cough at the time. "It was a powerful experience to see Joanne treat Roger with TFT diagnostic procedures and watch his recovery over the days. I had amazing experiences of TFT helping me personally. It was so calming." J

It was on this diagnostic training that Ian Graham, who was assisting on the course, suggested, "You must pursue music and TFT, it has not been done before by others - start seriously thinking about a self-help book, TFT and music."

The day after the training, I attended the inspirational and very unique 'TFT meets NLP' event. It was the only time when Roger Callahan - founder of TFT, Richard Bandler - co-creator of Neuro Linguistic Programming NLP and the hypnotist Paul McKenna, were on stage together sharing their wisdom and techniques.

---

[2] My article Toxins Tics and Toes was published in *Tapping the Body's Energy Pathways* by Dr Roger Callahan 2011.

Here I learned from a question asked by a member of the audience, that using TFT can enhance your abilities - even if, for example, you are dyslexic. I returned home from this training with an inner sense of calm.

In 2005 I left Buxlow School, marking the end of my music class teaching career.

My last employed work was with the Young Music Makers at Hendon Music Centre. When in 2006 I went for my interview with Sharon Broughall, the head of the centre, I immediately explained my interest in using TFT to help musicians. Effectively I went there as Rosemary Wiseman plus TFT, as I could no longer separate my music and therapeutic skills; the results I was getting with musicians were too good. I introduced TFT as part of the programme of the Young Music Makers - small groups of children aged between four and seven. Some children, and later some adults I worked with, even came to know me as the 'tapping lady'.

I was also given the opportunity to demonstrate TFT to the teenagers in their large wind band, a most challenging, yet positive experience.

At home with my private music students, I was so amazed by the results I was achieving through using TFT that I began making recordings of some of them, before and after the tapping sequences. I did this as I realised it could be hard for anyone to believe what was possible in improving musical performance so rapidly.

When I returned to Trinity College of Music, which had now relocated to Greenwich, I gave talks and demonstrations for the students during Freshers' Week for a number of years. (In 2005 Trinity Laban Conservatoire of Music and Dance was formed as a merger of Trinity College of Music and Laban Dance Centre.) It was natural for me to want to share what I had learned about using TFT with musicians and music students. One year I found myself doing an online test for dyslexia and attending talks by others on complementary techniques. If only these had been available when I was at Music College. If only there had been TFT when I was at Music College. My goal was to bring TFT techniques to music students through the book you are reading now.

Apart from my talks and demonstrations of TFT, I wrote articles for various publications including The British Thought Field Therapy Association *BTFTA Journal* and the Callahan Techniques'

Thought Field Newsletters, the Association of Thought Field Therapy *ATFT Update*, *The National Council for Hypnotherapy (NCH) Journal* and another hypnotherapy journal called *The Fountain.*

Then in May 2006 I presented my findings at the BTFTA and ATFT joint conference in Leamington Spa; I also demonstrated how very quickly I could help many people learn to sing in tune. That day quite a number of delegates discovered they had a voice they had not previously believed they had!

'The conference started with a presentation by Rosemary Wiseman.' She explained that 'After TFT, musicians were usually more relaxed and found that they could concentrate better, which was better for a good performance. They often reported that it was easier to play their music and performing then became more enjoyable. Rosemary herself said, "There is much untapped musical potential out there!" '[3]

I was very fortunate to again meet Dr Roger Callahan and Joanne Callahan at this conference. I really appreciated their interest in keeping TFT as simple and as accessible to all as possible. Roger was particularly interested in the work I was doing with musicians: *"Let me know if I can be of any help to you."* I replied that he already was, as he was always willing to reply to my emails, talk to me on the phone, or even assist with a music student or client.

I treasured our email exchanges and saved them in a document, which was fortunate because, as I found, emails from time ago can get automatically deleted.

After the conference Roger emailed me:
"5.7.06: Thank you so much. I really enjoy hearing and watching your brilliant use of TFT to help your musical clients.

Again, many thanks,
Roger"

When I emailed Roger about the only 'reversal', and its possible cause, in my presentation, "how we turn those good days into bad

---

[3] BTFTA and ATFT Joint Conference Report BTFTA Newsletter, September 2006.

days" Roger replied *"Great awareness. We usually are blinded to such utterances."*

When I began to find out how TFT could help with musical performance, one of my colleagues was stunned into silence. Thinking that this could just be some strange new idea of little value, they asked me, "Where is it all going?" Well with this book, it is going far and I thank you for becoming part of its journey.

In these seven chapters, I have been pleased to share with you the succession of turning points, which have led me to where I am. Now I would like to present you with a series of situations where I have used TFT tapping and other techniques, including ideas I have developed myself, with various musicians and music students to help them on their musical way.

Zoom 2

Calmer teaching and performing

Chapter 8
Theme and variations
A-Z handbook of music lessons and ideas
for practical music making

A
A for AFFIRMATIONS when performing

'The most important words you'll ever hear are those you tell yourself.' Dr Brian Roet

You can perform best when you are thinking positively and are focused and absorbed in the music itself. After a good performance, one of my students described her state while she was playing her instrument:

"I am only thinking about the music and how it goes."

This is much more useful than "I think I am going to make a mistake."

Make up your own affirmations. Keep them in the first person, in the present tense and positive.

Here are some examples my students have made up:
"I can remember this."
"I can do it."
"When I am performing a piece, *I KEEP GOING*."

For reading ahead in Sight Reading:
"I am focusing on looking forward."

A also for Be My ACCOMPANIST

If you are a piano teacher who plays other musical instruments, you can instantly transform your piano student into an accompanist. The student plays a well-known or repertoire piece and you play the melody line, or even a harmony line on a different instrument. This can teach so many aspects of music and is likely to be both a challenging and rewarding experience for the student.

B

B for BE SURE

Where I notice a student 'guessing' something about music in their lesson, I write in their notebook the word 'GUESS' and then cross it out. Guessing is literally ruled out. In music there is always an answer somewhere.

HOPE is a more rarely expressed word in music performance:

"Did you do the *time saver* (play the music correctly)?" I ask my student Alec.
"I hope so" he replies.

Of all the words written by me that you are reading in this book, the 'hope' word is one you will only find in this section.

How do we get from THINK SO or HOPE SO, to KNOW SO?
How do we get from NOT SURE to BE SURE?

If after using the *successipe* - a recipe for successful practice (more about this later) - you are still confused about what you are playing, it may only be that you are learning something new. When you are not sure a*sk useful questions* of yourself or your teacher.

Take Time - T.T. Take one thing at a time that you want to work on. Use the *ZOOM lesson, say play, key notes* or do a *slow lesson* and see if you can work it out for yourself. If you are still not sure and you are alone, leave it to your next lesson, maybe marking the music with a question mark in pencil.

"Can you show me how this music goes? If you do not, I will only end up going on YouTube." Adult student

It can be helpful at times to know what to aim for. Your teacher may play or sing a phrase so that you know how the music is supposed to go. Personally I make sure the musical notation has at first been understood.

For example, if I think a student is guessing, as they are naming a note incorrectly, I ask them, 'How do you know that? How do you know it is correct?'

Once you are SURE, repetitive practice can begin. The worst that can happen is you are wrong and do not notice your mistake.

B also for BUILDING

Helmet – put your thinking cap on
Scaffolding – Support will be needed

Focus on one thing at a time. Like it was suggested to me with the writing of this book, so with music: build the house one room - one chapter, one part, one bit - at a time. You can always go back and add more decorations later.

Student comments: *"This lesson was good. In the past I used to keep going, making mistakes."*

C

C also for CHAIN TEACHING

"While we teach, we learn," said the Roman philosopher Seneca.

Teaching something that you have learned recently to someone else will reinforce your learning. It could be teaching a younger sibling, friend or even a parent. (I first taught school friends piano and recorder.)

C also for CHOOSE A LESSON

Make a pack of cards. On one side of the card write the names of a variety of music lessons in this book, such as B for Be Sure.

Turn the cards over to the 'blank' side and mix them up. The teacher, or the student, can then choose a card at random from the pack. Alternatively, choose one directly from this book and see how it can apply and be useful to you.

D

D for DO IT NOW

E

E for ENERGY

The tips here are helpful for overcoming tiredness or excessive yawning during a lesson and can be used at home for practice as well.

It can be useful to know when a student arrives for their lesson if they are particularly low in energy.

Here are a number of ways you can help increase energy rapidly:

- Musical Instrument – even a few minutes of playing your musical instrument can energise you. If it does not, stop and do something different, perhaps some other form of relaxation.
- Drink water – this has quickly stopped the yawning or raised energy by several points in my students; with 0 being the least energy and 10 the most.
  If you are thirsty it is 'too late', it means you are dehydrated.
- TFT – tap PR spot (side of hand) or *collarbone breathing* CB2 if necessary, see Appendix.
- Get up, stretch and move around.
- Consider diet or supplements.

E also for ENJOYMENT – 'The Pleasurometer'

Find out how much students have enjoyed their practice and their lesson. How much do they enjoy their pieces?

E also for EXPECTATIONS

Expectations can be high from both teacher and student alike. Check out your expectations and those of your student as you consider the following:

- Progress
- Enjoyment
- Expect less or more. Do you need to raise or lower the bar?
- Do more
- Balance your expectations

When expectations to achieve have been too high, take easy steps;

make things as *easy* as you can. This will help restore confidence.

If expectations have become too high for you to achieve what you want, just do the best you can at the time.

Have high expectations of your students, yet keep an open mind. After all, unless they tell us or we ask, we may not know what is happening or what has taken place in the life of our student since their last lesson. One student was not performing as well as usual and there seemed to be no apparent reason. Later that day she sent me a text to say she had forgotten to tell me that she had been involved in a car accident earlier in the day!

On the other hand, it can be useful to expect more from our students. By motivating them to achieve more, there can be some surprises and this can also lead to greater confidence and progress.

F

F for FIVE FINGER EXERCISE for pianists

This exercise is a 'hand me down' from my own piano teacher, Eva Bernathova. It is helpful for finger strengthening and developing curved fingers, whilst keeping a flexible wrist.

Relax the shoulders - flop your hands onto the piano keys and allow your arms to hang loosely by the sides of the piano stool.

Where necessary, correct your positioning and repeat the steps below:

Step 1 - KNEES
Working very slowly with one hand at a time, put your hand around your knee.

Step 2 - KEYS
Keeping your hand in this position, place it over five consecutive keys of the piano keyboard; for example, C - G. Check whether your fingers are still curved. When you see that they are, continue on to the next step.

Step 3 - PRESS
Again, keeping the same position, lower your hand gently and silently onto the keys. Check your fingers are still curved. When you see that they are, continue on to the next step.

Step 4 – PLAY
Taking each of your five fingers in turn, beginning with the first piano finger, i.e. the thumb, raise then lower the finger on to the keys in a natural way. Repeat this action a few times, very slowly, ensuring that all the fingers remain curved.

F also for FREEZE!

As the student plays their piano piece, suddenly the teacher calls out FREEZE! The student can then look at their hand position. Is it correct?

F also for FUNNY STORIES

Sharing some funny stories, musical ones if you have them, can be a very useful and quick way to help a young student get into a better state if they have arrived for their music lesson feeling upset.

Laughter is known to be very healing and is beneficial to learning. Find a way to incorporate it in your lessons if you do not already do so.

G

G for GOALPOSTS – WE BOTH MOVE THEM

The teacher guides their student with suggestions about what to prepare and practise for their next lesson. Success involves setting a realistic and achievable plan. Adjust the goalposts to suit.

H

H for HANDS SEPARATELY piano lesson

Having a lesson only playing hands separately, can remove the urge to put the hands together too soon. It can also help demonstrate how essential it is to practise hands separately, even when the music is known quite well.

Student comments on the benefits of this lesson:

"I had not practised hands separately as I had 'no time'.

Now I realise it is worth it, as I can play the music correctly. It speeds up your progress and also helps you to memorise, which makes playing easier."

I

I for I CAN

This lesson is very effective for confidence building.

It helps to get rid of self-limitations and reminds us of what we CAN do.

For example,

I can…give myself reasonable expectations

I can…keep going when I make a mistake

There is usually a remarkable difference in the student when they have their next lesson.

In my very early days of teaching piano, one of my students was my nephew Jonathan. In desperation, I told him that when he said 'I can't' for the tenth time, I would have to stop the lesson, which is exactly what happened. I did not have the tools that I have now and did not know how to help him over this at the time.

In the I CAN lesson I get students to think about what they *can* do, possibly quite unrelated to music at first. I begin to list these in their notebook and then suggest they continue this process at home; they can fill up an imaginary confidence pot before they go to sleep with all the things they *can* do. Self-praise is very important and often underused.

J

J for JIGSAW

Music lessons can at times feel like a *jigsaw*, as we fit together all the bits of the pieces that have been practised or work out what still needs more practice.

K

K for KEEP FIT

There are many ways to keep emotionally as well as physically fit, according to an individual's preferences; from walking, to swimming, or other simple exercises such as tapping a TFT sequence. This is very important for a musician. In this book I highlight some techniques which I have found most useful myself, as well as with helping other musicians.

L

L for LEARNING: THE A -------------- B LINE

This is the journey from the first and early stages of l*earning* music to the *performing* stage. Just as in life, along it you are always learning and always performing in some ways.

'A' - the learning stage: Aim for excellence. Here you are thinking carefully so as to get the music 'perfect' and correct - particularly when learning classical music.

This is the foundation, like 'nursery'.[1] There is much repetition at this stage.

'B' - The Performing stage, like 'university' level: Be your best. Here you need to let go of being 'perfect' and trust yourself, your fingers or your memory.

As you go along the learning line, which is always moving, you keep learning and will get better at whatever you are practising.

Notice what is hard? What made it easier and how did this happen? Use these ideas to improve your learning.

If you are stuck, seek to find out what is causing this. Maybe adjusting the tempo could help. Or maybe you need to go back to 'A' – the *learning* stage, when you first started your learning. Now you are likely to move along the *Learning Line* much faster as you progress towards 'university' - the *performing* stage.

M

M for M.A.W. – Music All the Way...

The theme of this book.

M also for MAKE IT EASY

Ask 'what would make it easier?'

M also for MEMORY

Learning to play from memory or 'by heart'.

Know the music so well that you can just play it off by heart naturally. This comes from a lot of repetition.

---

[1] *Don't shoot the dog*! The new art of teaching and training by Karen Pryor published by Ringpress Books Ltd 2002

Another way is to play short sections and later the whole piece:
1. With the music
2. Without the music
3. With the music

M also for MUF -
The musical triangle of communication

The **Music**, **U** (you) and your **Fingers**
Think of it like this: **Music** = rules, **U** = referee, **F** = players

Music: Musical notation is like the rules, **U** You are the referee and your **Fingers** are the players. Teamwork is essential.

The **Music** tells **U** what to play; now **U** tell your **Fingers** what to play. Using **MUF** can help with music reading and improving the geography of playing your instrument.

Mind your Fingers – they have a mind of their own.

The **Music** requires **U** to play the note C, yet your **Fingers** may seem to want to play an F. *Be Sure* your fingers are playing what is written in the music.

Sometimes in the **Music**, **U** may need to be bossy and *direct* your **Fingers**. Contrary to this, there comes a time when there will be a need for **U** to 'get out of way' and simply *trust* your **Fingers**. For example, on playing a scale one student said, "when I think about it, it goes wrong." This is where **U** are getting in the way and not trusting your fingers.

The process of MUF happens slowly when there is little trust in your fingers as yet. Let us call this 'slow MUF'.

When the process of MUF happens very quickly - 'Fast MUF' - there is complete trust - automatic ability. Torvill and Dean, the British ice dancers and former British, European and Olympic World champions, describe this as a place where they 'get lost in it'.

As one of my students said, "I can let my fingers take over from my brain. Then I can switch off and do it from muscle memory."

N

N for a NINETY SECONDS PRACTICE
Natalie's ninety second practice
See Chapter 11 - Improve your practising

O

O for OVER PRACTICE

P

P for PROGRESS
It is essential for both student and teacher to know that progress is being made. Measure your progress and success.

The Progress Line 0_____10
Assess this before, during and at the end of the lesson
How much do you think you have progressed since your last music lesson? Was your playing better than last time? How can you be certain you have progressed? What challenges did you have along the way? What can be improved?

As one is striving to improve and progress, it is also important and useful to appreciate what has been achieved in the past. Going back to playing and relearning an old piece can be a good way to do this.

Student comments - Josie Woolf
"It doesn't really matter, as I keep going and progressing, however slowly. Some weeks may be slower than others, some faster than others." Josie always encouraged other players to 'keep going'.

Q

Q for QUIET TIME

R

R for REPERTOIRE

 Always have pieces in your repertoire, preferably including some by heart, which you can play well at short notice.

R also for RHYTHM - COUNTING ALOUD

To help play a rhythm accurately, where needed, *clap* the rhythm of the musical notation as you *count* the beats *aloud*.

For wind players, afterwards you can play this rhythm on your instrument as you count in your head.

Pianists, string players and percussionists can *play and count aloud* at the same time. Some piano students find it more difficult to co-ordinate this and will have to play more slowly. Collarbone breathing can be helpful for this, see Appendix.

When you 'say' the sounds of the rhythm of the notes, whether using the French Time Names (for example Ta, Ta - a) or numbers, or a combination, it helps you to learn more easily as you are really hearing what you are playing. Most benefit is achieved when there is a focus on actively *listening* to what you are counting aloud. Later you can count in your head. One of my students called it 'muted counting'. This can be easier and faster, even if not always so accurate at first for some.

S

S for SILENT MUSIC TEACHING (MIMING)

This lesson came about (in 2002) when a student kept looking at me for reassurance as to how well they had played their music on the piano. I would show them the smiley face of a paper plate when they played well - I just happened to have one of those plates in my room at the time. When something in the playing needed to be improved, I began to write some suggestions on the back of the plate and point to these. On the day I had temporarily lost my voice, the silent music teacher lesson was born.

The back of the plate:

1. Slow
2. Notes (MUF)
3. Fingering
4. Rhythm – Counting aloud
5. Dynamics and articulation
6. Concentration
7. Beat
8. Speed
9. Listen
10. Look at the music
11. Do you like this piece? 1-10
12. Now practise! Zoom 88, Time Savers, Say Play

Student comments:
"It makes me more independent." "I had to work harder and think faster.

S also for your SIXTH SENSE – PROPRIOCEPTION

Train your musical brain and develop proprioception, your sixth sense. It is an essential skill for sight-reading.

Pianists - keep your eyes on the music and avoid looking at the piano keyboard. Sometimes I hold a thin music book above students' hands, so that they cannot see their fingers when they are playing the piano. This helps with music reading and keyboard geography - how notes on the piano can be found without needing to look. Another way to improve keyboard geography is to close your eyes when playing, or play in the dark. Children particularly enjoy impressing their parents with this. Observing a colleague sight-reading one day, I noticed how little they needed to look at their fingers. When did you last have the opportunity to observe another pianist sight-reading?

S also for SPOT

The teacher plays a well-known song (even one of the student's pieces) on a musical instrument of their choice, and 'accidentally' plays a wrong note. The student raises their hand or calls out as soon as they notice this. Then the student plays one of their pieces and 'accidentally' plays a wrong note. Now it is the teacher's turn to notice this. It is a fun game; good for getting any student into a better state where needed at the beginning of a lesson and is also very useful for assessing and improving aural.

S also for SURPRISE, SURPRISE!

I love surprises. I suggest my students give me a surprise in one lesson. In another, I will give *them* a surprise. My favourite surprises are when students make exceptional progress from one lesson to the next, or they learn a new piece by themselves, which I am not expecting. Sometimes I invite them to give me such a surprise.

With certain students I have done some rather unusual things as a surprise to help them with their learning or with their fears; to get them over performance nerves or simply to feel more comfortable in the lesson.

One of my students had a fear of heights, as well as performing. One piano lesson began with a visit to our balcony, which helped her get over her phobia. When she came for her next piano lesson I asked her how her performance on the piano had gone. 'It was good.' She told me. 'Now I am not afraid of anything.'

T

T for TALK TO YOUR TEACHER
Ask questions
This is informative and useful for both students and parents. Parents, where possible, please do this at the beginning rather than the end of lessons. There are some students that find talking to their teacher very natural. Others are more reserved.

One student was keen to get the music for her next grade, yet did not like to ask me directly as she was 'mind reading' the answer I might give. Remember, you or the parent can *ask your teacher* about anything in the *talk to your teacher lesson.*

One student even asked, "What happens in the '*ask your teacher* or *talk to your teacher'* lesson?" Just asking this question helped them to realise, there was no need to have any fears in future about asking me any questions.

It can be that you want to ask questions or talk about your lessons, your musical goals, or indeed anything else. Some students need no such invitation for this lesson. Better this than the case of a student who told me that her previous piano teacher was so terrifying that she was too scared to ask her if she could throw away a tissue in the bin. Needless to say she did not continue lessons with this teacher.

Like my wearing of slippers, following in the footsteps of Dr Brian Roet, I also have objects in my music room that encourage some questions. It is just a matter of time before a student asks:

"Why do you have a smiley face ornament on your piano?"

"When you smile you relax" I reply.

Tell your teacher
Which pieces you like best or least.
Why you do not like some pieces.
What you find difficult or what is easy.

This could help you as their teacher decide to write O.M.W. - One More Week to work on this piece, as it is not their favourite.

Tell your teacher how much or little you have practised. The *Weekly Rhythm Record* makes this easy to do.

Tell your teacher what and how you have practised, for example what you have focused on.

What do you enjoy or like most about your lessons?

Answers can be informative or even amusing and have included:

'Your fun ideas.'

'Your dog…and you! Or, 'You…and your dog.'

'With you I am learning with love. You are so encouraging. Piano lessons with my previous teacher used to take place in a freezing cold dark room where everything was neat and proper. I like the light; the comfortable room and the toys all around represent happiness.'

One young piano student was distracted by my box of hand-held percussion instruments. There was no need to ask what they liked the most about their piano lesson.

What do you like least about your lessons?

Answers have included:

'The left hand on the piano; it is difficult.'

'When I go wrong.'

T also for TEACH ME

This is when the teacher changes places with their student and asks them to 'teach me' something they are currently learning on their instrument. Students love giving their teacher a lesson. The teacher, in their new role as 'student', will of course 'accidentally' make some mistakes.

T also for TRYING

Some students overuse the word *try*. With these students I replace it with alternative and more positive words.

I cross the word 'TRY' out in students' notebooks as it implies failure. Instead I write, JUST DO IT, or PLAY IT depending on what is appropriate.

Here is a short version of how I demonstrate the '*try*' word.

Do it for yourself right now:

Try to pick up a pen or take a pen from your teacher as they hand it to you.

What did you just do?

Just take or pick up the pen? Was it easier (than trying)?

Or *try* to stand up.

What did you just do?

Just stand up? Was it easier (than trying)?

Have you ever *tried* to relax? It is easier just to relax.

SLOWING DOWN can help.

Take one bit at a time

At home or going about your daily life, notice if you are in a *trying* state - where you are '*trying*' to do something. What is that task?

Student comments: "I just do what I know I can do"

U

U for USEFUL QUESTIONS

Ask yourself or your teacher useful questions such as:

What am I focusing on?

Am I using the correct, or suggested, fingering?

Am I playing the correct notes?

Am I playing the correct notes in the correct time?

Am I using the correct hands?

Which note do I start on?

Which bar needs extra practice?

What makes learning a new piece easier?

How much should I practise?

How can I remember a scale?

How can I be sure I am playing the correct notes?

The answers to your questions will be helped by the suggestions, methods and techniques in this book.

V

V for VIRTUOSO, aim to be the best

This 'theme' for a lesson is different from all the others in this book in that the title itself came first.[2]

What is a virtuoso?

---

[2] Idea from my author-friend Kevin Desmond

Which virtuoso musicians have you heard or seen perform live?
Can you describe your experience as you listened to them?

If you were aiming to be a *virtuoso*, aiming to be the best, what would you do to prepare yourself from one music lesson to the next? How would you prepare yourself for a performance?

For one student, aged nine, her classmate who is on Grade 6 is like a *virtuoso*. For another, aged six, it is her mother, who inspired her to learn the piano in the first place. For others it may be you, their teacher.

W

W for WARM-UP

It is very useful to give students a short time, on their own where appropriate, to warm up on their instrument and get comfortable in the room. I introduced it into my lessons as my students told me they liked having this included. It was something that I appreciated having with one of my teachers when I was studying.

It can be interesting for the teacher to listen to what their students play in the warm-up time when they can play anything they want. It can also help the teacher to identify any practice methods that could be improved.

X

X for 'X-Ray Eyes' are needed for studying the music.

Y

Y for WHY?

Why do you want to learn and play music?

Z

Z for ZOOM!

Look carefully at the current exam syllabus to ensure you or your student are complying with the current requirements; in particular, the pieces, scales and supporting tests. The story of a certain candidate, who I was accompanying for her Grade 8 bassoon exam, comes to mind. When she arrived at my home for the first rehearsal, I discovered that one of her pieces was not on the exam list. She quickly had to prepare a different one.

Chapter 9
Slow is fast progress

SLOW

S for THE SLOW LESSON

"Practise slowly at home. Here, in your lesson, it is already too late. There is no other way. I think that those who do not believe me and do not practice slowly, will never make it. Most people do not have the patience to practise slowly." Eva Bernathova.

In this chapter I will share with you some ways you can slow down when needed and master slow practice. I feel well qualified to do this as a student of Eva. She would sometimes say to me, "*your* slow and *my* slow are two different things." (A few of my own students will find these words familiar.) Like the tortoise, I can do slow and am naturally fast in certain ways as well.

Slow or *slowly* were the most frequent words I found myself using prior to teaching the *slow lesson.* Slow practice is essential when learning and practising music, yet for many students it can be difficult. They may even be unable to experience the value of it. Perhaps this is due to the fast pace of our lives or the desire to be able to learn and play a piece or a passage of music immediately, without putting in the necessary work.

Teaching *slow practice* can be a real challenge as well. One day it took me thirty minutes to help a young piano student slow down. Each time they made a mistake, I suggested they needed to play it a little slower. I thought there must be a quicker way to get a student to slow down, so I began to use other methods to achieve this rather than continually using the *slow* word.

Ask yourself these questions:

How quickly can I slow down?
What helps me to slow down?

One of my Grade 7 piano students, Vicky, found it very difficult to slow down and continually made errors. I explained to her that some teachers, like my piano teacher Eva, who was professor of piano at Trinity College of Music, had even refused to teach a student at the college because they were unable to slow down as instructed. The challenge was on for us both as I offered Vicky one of my *slow lessons*.

"That is going to be painful," she said fearfully. "I do not like going slowly all the time. I can only do it in small bursts."

I played her one of the recordings I had made of all the pieces I had learned when studying piano with Eva. What I noticed most on listening to them again more recently, was that through them I could retrace what I had learned through Eva: slow practice pays off. The music was not played at the fastest of speeds, yet it was clear, accurate, expressive and above all, enjoyable to listen to (a joy which some musicians are unable to experience when listening to their own recordings). Using my recording to convey these elements to Vicky was powerful. I was as delighted as she was when - after the lesson - Vicky realised that she now had enough control to slow down immediately.

Some teachers get frustrated when their students keep making mistakes. I always remember when Dame Fanny Waterman, in her mid-nineties, gave her most informative and inspiring pedagogical lecture and master classes at the Oxford Piano Festival. One of these master classes was with some of her younger students. To one of them she put it in a nutshell:

"You are making the same mistake because you are practising too fast." Dame Fanny then demonstrated how *slow* gives you *listening time*.

The *slow lesson* may even include a variety of slowed - down actions. Different ideas will work for different people. Simply suggesting certain words like *twice as slow, super-slow* or *slow-motion* can be effective.

The mother of an eight-year-old piano student of mine gave her daughter a reminder band - bracelet - with the words *slow down* on it to support what she was learning in this lesson. She has now even gone up the rankings in her class, showing how the benefits of such music lessons can affect other areas in life, such as schoolwork, or managing stress.

The fastest progressing students are the ones who go slowest when practising or learning new music.

SLOWEST playing – FASTEST progress

LESS IS MORE

Here are a number of other techniques and ideas that I developed over time, as I became a *'musical slow coach'*. They can be used individually or in combination as part of a *slow lesson*.

Choose from the following suggestions after your student has played some music where you felt they were rushing or out of control, because they were playing too fast. Afterwards you can notice or ask: How different is the performance of the same music now?

B for BREATHING
When preparing a school production I was directing, a parent of one of the children involved said to me.

"I bet you haven't got time to breathe!" Sometimes it takes someone else to remind us of this most effective approach to slowing down – *breathing*.

Breathe slowly – breathe in 'calm' and release any tension as you breathe out. Do this now. How does it feel?

See diaphragmatic breathing Chapter 5 and Appendix Look after your voice.

B also for BAKING LESSON
See Chapter 11 Improve your practising

C for THE CANARY LESSON
See Chapter 11 Improve your practising

F for PLAY IT FAST
Have some fun - suggest to your student that they play a piece of music faster than you think they can manage. What can you learn or discover from this?

F for FiveQT
Five minutes *Quiet Time*.
Stop! Stop what you are doing right now. Take a few moments or minutes of *quiet time* before continuing. In *FiveQT* the student sits quietly alone for five minutes (adjust time to suit age or requirements) neither playing their instrument nor doing any other task.

Slowing down reduces anxiety.

SLOW = CALM

H for MUSICAL HANGMAN
In my search for different and effective ways to help music students who rush their practice or performance, I have been known to play this game of hangman with them, in a music lesson. It is a fun way to emphasise the importance of these words:
Extra slowly gives us

- - - -   - -   - - - - - about - - - - - - - - - - - -

(time to think about lots of things)

Now play a piece of music slowly and notice just which musical aspects you have time to think about.

M for AN UNUSUAL USE OF A METRONOME

I can still see my metronome sitting on top of my grand piano when I was a child. I hear it going tic tic tic, with my sister Vivienne saying, "If you are going to play with it, at least play in time with it."

Some years after discovering through Dr Brian Roet[1] that a metronome can help reduce performance anxiety, I began using one with my students to improve their musical performance; I found that it helped them to slow down.

Find out for yourself how effective a metronome can be:
Keep a note of the numbers – Beats Per Minute (BPM) used at all stages.
1.   Set the metronome to a random number - BPM.
2.   Allow it to be heard for a few moments.
3.   Ask if this feels comfortable for the student, or is it too fast or slow? Keep asking this question as you continue.
4.   Adjust the BPM until they do feel comfortable. If the chosen tempo is fast, considerably over 60 beats per minute (BPM), gradually reduce the number; you may even set one that is too slow for them, until they feel comfortable and calmer with this.

P for POETRY

Recite a quote or poem about slowing down sourced from the Internet.

'Slow down and enjoy life. It's not only the scenery you miss by going too fast - you also miss the sense of where you are going and why.' Eddie Cantor

S for SAY PLAY

See the *successipe* Chapter 11

---

[1] The Confidence to be Yourself – Dr Brian Roet Published by Judy Piatkus (Publishers) Limited 1998

S also for THE MUSICAL SECRET-ARY
See Chapter 11 *Improve your practising*

Through this game, some students slow down automatically. Others will need to learn how to slow down to ensure that they play the music correctly.

S also for THE SHOPPING lesson

Here is some food for thought:
In the same way that you may pause to read labels before making a purchase in a supermarket, you need to pause and read musical 'labels' - musical symbols - for example, the key signature.

S also for SLOW TEACHING
Do you ever find you are as excited as your students about their desire to achieve certain goals? It is an interesting experience for us as teachers to slow down ourselves and do some *slow teaching*: allow the student to master each tiny step before moving on.
Teach slowly (do a *slow lesson*) and observe the effects.
Teach fast (do a *fast lesson*) and observe the effects.

T .T. for TAKE TIME
This is essential when you are learning something new. Tell your student of the experience you are currently having with something new you are learning in life.

Take Time T.T before you start a piece and think about the music you are about to play.

T also for TEMPO GIUSTO[2]
Play music at the speed that you can perform it well. When you are learning and practising new music, adjust and find your *own speed – tempo giusto*. Play it as slowly as necessary in order to play accurately. This helps accelerate learning.

---

[2] In Praise of Slowness – Carl Honoré HarperCollins Publishers 2004

T also for THOUGHT FIELD THERAPY (TFT)
See Appendix

Tapping the PR spot, (the side of the hand) 10 to 20 times, or tapping sequences, such as for anxiety or fear, can rapidly calm and slow the anxious performer down.

T also for TIME SAVERS
At first you may feel that you are slowing down while you work on *time savers.* However, they will help you to learn your music faster. See the *successipe* Chapter 11.

Z for ZOOM! See the *successipe* Chapter 11.

* * *

Remember the story of The Tortoise and the Hare

* * *

Student comments on benefits of the *slow lesson*:

"It is one of my favourite lessons."

"Playing slowly or slow practice gives you time to think, concentrate, focus, listen and look at the music."

"Slow is easier, it gives you time to do the *time savers*."

"It is good; I know I can get the notes right."

"You can hear what you are playing. When you are playing fast you do not pick up on your mistakes. You can focus on how you play, not just the notes."

"When I did the slow lesson I got everything right and I feel happy and proud."

"It was relaxing and made me feel really calm".

"I used to practise the guitar too fast. I learned through the *slow lesson* on the piano to practise slowly".

"I think we should have this lesson more often".

'It is much easier as you have time to get your bearings and everything else works from that.'

"I can always get faster later. It is better to get the correct notes the first time."

* * *

Use the slow lesson and find out how well it works for you.

Chapter 10
A first piano lesson

Varying amounts of this lesson can be covered, according to your students readiness to learn.

Have they ever played the piano before?

Listen to anything that they can play.

Improvisation is encouraged from the very beginning.

Explore some of the basic elements of music on the piano and observe which concepts are known. Teach any concepts that need to be understood.

R for **R**hythm   - long and short
S for **S**peed   - fast and slow
V for **V**olume   - loud and soft
P for **P**itch   - high and low

Thumb is 1

Play with the rhythm Long, long, long, short long, long, long.

The fingering is 111 2345

This teaches a number of different skills, from the finger numbers on the hand and legato playing, to listening and co-ordination.

Say *Thumb is 1* aloud to the above rhythm, while playing on the piano. You can start on any note. First with the right hand, then the left hand and finally hands together in contrary motion.

Thumb is 1, hold it down - if necessary, with 'musical (pretend) glue' - then play 2. Build it up until all five fingers can be played in the correct rhythm.

Use to encourage simple improvisation.

A variation for some can be 5554321 in the same rhythm as Thumb is 1.

The Siren or **Nee Nor** as some young children call it.
212121 (finger numbers of the right hand)
This is a fun sound effect to develop legato playing and get the fingers working. Some students naturally start to use other fingers - 323232.

The Piano Keyboard
The black keys on the piano, once described by a young beginner of mine as "lollipops in a line" need to be seen as a pattern of two and three.

Find a group of two black notes, then a group of three black notes. Now find more of each of these groups. Being able to follow these instructions is a good indicator of how ready the student is to learn the keyboard.

The *Froggy Jumps* are a successful method I developed for teaching the letter names of the notes on the keyboard.

Teach Me. Young students love to teach their parents the *Froggy Jumps* and observe their difficulty in learning, or 'pretend struggles' if they can already play the instrument.

If the student has learned piano before, look for signs that the *Froggy Jumps* could be helpful to speed up their ability to find notes. For example:
- They are counting from middle C to find various notes
- They are giving incorrect answers to questions about finding and naming notes.

FROGGY JUMPS
Group 1
C is on the left of **two black notes**
D is in the middle of **two black notes**
E is on right of **two black notes**

Group 2
F is on the left of **three black notes**
B is on the right of **three black notes**

Group 3
G is on the right of F
A is on the left of B

With each group in turn, play all the C's on the piano, then all the D's, then all the E's and so on.

Now mix the letters up; for example, play a C high up on the piano, a D in the middle or low down on the piano and so on. Once this is achieved very quickly, go on to the next group, until you can mix the letters up of all three groups.

Chant or make up songs to help with learning the words for the *Froggy Jumps*. For example, *C is on the left of two black notes.*

Pieces or songs

Playing music from written musical notation, either using a tutor book, your own material or a combination. Personally I like the *Me and My Piano* series first published by Faber in 1988, latest edition 2008, as fingering *time savers* are used in moderation compared to some other tutor books.

From the beginning, encourage students to focus on one thing at a time:

1. SAY PLAY – SAY the letter name (ABC...) of the note aloud, then PLAY it.
2. COUNT ALOUD – count the beats of the rhythm aloud.

For counting the rhythm with beginners, some of the French Time Names are included:

♩ = Crotchet = 1 beat = ta

𝅗𝅥 = Minim = 2 beats = ta-a

𝅗𝅥. = Dotted minim = 3 beats =123

o = Semibreve = 4 beats =1234

♫ = Quavers = two half beat notes = ta te

3. Other elements as appropriate, such as fingering, articulation or the words of the song.

Although this lesson is aimed at beginners, certain parts of it can be used with more advanced students, particularly if you have 'inherited' them from another teacher, or they have previously been self-taught.

Chapter 11
Improve your practising
A-Z handbook on learning and practising music

A Grade 3 student once said to me, *"you have taught me how to practise. I wasn't taught this before."*
Consider the following two questions, the first of which both teachers and parents are often more concerned about:

How much have you practised?
How have you practised?

What a difference the omission of one word can make on the subject of practice. *How* you practise is just as important as *how much* you practise.
Here is a more unusual and good question from a parent of one of my students:
"Is my daughter practising in the right way?"
Have *you* ever been asked to 'do more' practice when you already felt you were doing 'the impossible'? This chapter will give you some ideas on how to improve the way you learn music, by practising and getting the best out of the time you and your students put into it.
How exactly do musicians practise and how can music teachers teach this?
Until this book was written, my husband Laurence did not know exactly how I teach. One day, while I was writing this chapter, he suggested this: "Why don't you show your students just how *you* would practise what they are working on?" In this A-Z on learning and practising, you will find many ways in which I do this.

A

A for ARMCHAIR PRACTICE

It was a wonderful opportunity - during the Oxford Piano Festival masterclass in 2014 - to pick up some tips from some of the talented participating students. One of them told me how he would study the music before playing a single note on the piano.

My version of this, the *armchair practice* lesson was already well established. The idea had come to me from conductors who studied music whilst travelling. This type of lesson has occasionally taken place in the armchair in my lounge, next to the room where I teach, though more frequently it would be on the piano stool. It can be used for the voice or any instrument. The following scenario was somewhat more unusual:

Today my 93-year-old mother Josie's piano music is on her lap as she sits in her armchair. I am wondering why the music is not on the piano stand in her room. Josie insists on putting her *Me and My Piano Part 2* music into a bag to take it into the garden with us. Why, I do not yet know.

Inspired after my recent *jigsaw* music lesson at her care home and keen to progress, Josie has been doing 'armchair practice' - studying her music from the comfort of her armchair. As we arrive in the garden, she carefully points to the musical notation. I am expecting her to be learning *Happy Birthday*, yet she does not want to miss out the previous piece - "I want to play the *Cuckoo*" she insists. Checking with me on some of the notes, I proceed to give her an 'armchair' piano lesson, in her wheelchair in the garden. The results a few days later showed the lesson had been successful, as Josie was able to play accurately what she had prepared that day in the garden.

The other preparation that can be done in the 'armchair' is to study your own practice recordings and other appropriate recordings. Just how even are your scales and fast passages of music? How could you make your music more expressive and meaningful?

B

B for BAKING LESSON
Share stories with your students about baking that went wrong. Talk about the importance of taking time to check ingredients in recipes and following them precisely for them to turn out well. Relate this to their learning and practising of music.

There are the cooking times - your practising times - and the different settings; these are the different ways you practise.

Following a recipe successfully – the *successipe*.

B also for BUILD UP PRACTICE
Practise in short sections. This can vary from one bar, a number of bars, a phrase or a part of the music. Once you can play the first section as accurately as you can at this stage, go on to the next one. Then join them up, depending on where they are located. Continue in this way until you have practised the complete piece. It is important when using this method to begin practising on different parts of the piece. Your first section may, for example, be the last eight bars of the piece.

C

C for THE CANARY LESSON
Have you ever had a student say that they play better when on their own at home?

Albeit that ducks are not canaries, let me tell you about an unusual experience, which paved the way for a very different kind of music teaching.

It was not the first time a piano lesson had been interrupted by a shared caring about wildlife birds. Once, as one of my adult students came into my house, we spotted a duck waddling past with a family of six ducklings. They were clearly on their way to a nearby lake. The piano lesson was delayed as we stopped passing traffic and escorted them safely over the busy main road at the end of my street.

The day my ten-year-old piano student, Jason, arrived for his lesson was somewhat different and one of the most unusual lessons I have ever taught. It was to change my teaching methods in an extraordinary and unexpected way. Jason's mother told me that she had spotted a yellow canary in the driveway of the house opposite us. It took us half - an - hour to get hold of the bird and find someone who could look after it.

By now it was the end of Jason's piano lesson, so I asked him to play me what he had been practising during this time. Taken aback and impressed by how well he had done and how much progress he had made, I asked what had helped him, as I had not been in the room. He told me it was because he only had a keyboard at home and this was the first time he had practised on a real piano. I explained to his mother how much difference this had made to Jason's practice. As a result his parents bought him a piano the following week.

This got me curious. How could I help my other students in a similar way? I began to experiment with a shortened version of *The Canary Lesson*, which only takes few minutes.

After giving the student some specific instructions about what to work on, I would leave the room, making them feel like they are practising 'at home'. Sometimes I might hear them and get insights about what happens when they practise alone; for example, whether they were practising mistakes. When I returned to the room, we would see how effective their practising had been, giving us both useful information on how to proceed with the lesson. If it had been particularly effective, as with Jason, we would look at what was different and why they had not done this at home. If their practising had been ineffective, I would give them an appropriate lesson such as the *Jigsaw*. Sometimes the best things happened with students progress when I left the room, as if by magic.

My cello student's playing often improved after a *canary lesson*. I discovered they did not have good practising techniques after all. A short discussion revealed some interesting information: 'It is much quieter here; there is more space. It helps me to concentrate. At home it is too noisy to practise.'

After a *canary lesson* with another student who was working towards her Grade 2 piano exam, I discovered she had been practising standing up at her keyboard. No wonder she did not want to practise for too long!

Interesting attitudes to practice can also be revealed, such as in this student's comments after a *canary lesson*:

"I'm a genius, because I practised the scales in 'canary time', usually I only practise what's essential."

One day a past piano student returned to me for a lesson. He was unprepared as he had been unable to practise. In true *canary lesson* style I left him to practise for a few minutes, expecting that he might have gone through quite a lot of the piece we had selected to work on. When I returned to the room, he had completed several bars to an excellent standard, having used approaches you will read about in this chapter. It was obvious he was one of my past students who had fully followed and taken on board what he had learned during previous lessons.

D
D for "THE MUSICAL DETECTIVE"

In her article on *eight tips for young pianists,* Dame Fanny Waterman refers to the need to be a *musical detective* and includes *musical detective* questions related to this in her *Me and My Piano* tutor book series.

As musicians, we are like *detectives* as we seek to recreate what has been composed in a piece of music; we guide our students to do likewise. So as a music student, being a *musical detective* will help you to become a better musician and perform well.

In this section of the book and the following chapters, there are plenty of *clues* which will help you with musical awareness, to concentrate, focus, look and listen to yourself and others, so you can get into '*Musical Detective Mode.*'

D also for DO IT NOW!

Overcoming Procrastination to practise
Make the time to practise.

E
E for ENJOYMENT – 'The Pleasurometer'

Students practise more when they like their pieces, get over any difficulties and are well motivated. Ask those all-important questions about enjoyment.

F

F for FUN IDEA(S) FOR YOUNG STUDENTS

The young student imagines they are the teacher and their class is watching and listening to them when they are practising at home.

I discovered this idea when one of my students kept saying, "*We've* practised this". Having an imaginary audience when practising will help simulate being 'on stage' and develop listening and performing skills.

F also for BE FUSSY

Listen with great care to your playing.
Produce the best sound you possibly can and then repeat it.

Ask yourself questions:
Can I play it better?
Was it better than before? Can I play it even better?

Ask your teacher questions about how you can play or improve the music.

G

G for GUIDED PRACTICE

Firstly, for three to five minutes, your student practises while you remain *silent* and *observe*. Notice how effective their practice has been. Then direct or guide your student's practice, if it is still needed, for a further three to five minutes.
What is the difference in techniques used?
What is the difference in results?
Which was most effective?

Here are some tips that emerged from introducing this lesson:
Read your lesson notebook.
Use the *successipe* image as a reminder.
Have the *successipe* chart in front of you.
The need of quiet space to practise.
Expectations
Be Fussy

Quality practice is best
Write in *time savers*
Be persistent
Leave what you are uncertain about.
Go over and over the music when you have played it correctly.

H

H for HOW (and WHAT)

I ask my students carefully chosen questions about *how* and what they have practised, for example:

"Did you practise it *hands separately, slowly,* or work on the *bits?* Did you use the *successipe?*"

"Have you just been playing your pieces straight through from the beginning until the end, once or twice or over and over again?"

"Did you practise this (piece) the most?"

"Did you just do a little practice on this (piece)?"

"Did you practise this (piece) at all?"

"Did you use the music at all when you practised this (piece) off by heart?"

I

I for THE INTERNET

The Internet is a wonderful tool and can aid practising when used wisely and selectively. Talk to your teacher and share.

J

J for JIGSAW

How do our students practise? Why have some of them not progressed as much as they could? Sometimes it can be like the missing pieces of a jigsaw. In a way I could say the whole of *Zoom88* has been like piecing together a musical jigsaw – of my life and work in music. The *jigsaw lesson* is an important part of this.

It began the day I happened to be starting a new jigsaw of 'The Symphony Orchestra', which I had set up on the table in our music room. There are many ways of starting a jigsaw. My preferred way is to begin with the outside borders, as it is relatively easy to find those straight parts of the individual pieces. As this task requires little concentration, I was about to use it for an unexpected and unusual purpose.

One of my piano students was having difficulties performing a piece in their lesson, yet every week they would say, "I have practised this." I started sorting the jigsaw pieces as I *observed* them work on it and *commented* on the most effective ways they could practise and progress. Achieving progress and success when practising in the lesson can be very motivating. Success leads to success.

The results were so impressive that I began to use a similar approach with other students who I thought might benefit from it, calling it a *jigsaw lesson*. It is also very useful for a student who has been unable to practise or who has not practised one particular piece or scale. The *jigsaw lesson* is a *guided practice lesson*, incorporating many of the techniques and ideas you are reading about in this book. You as the teacher 'step back' and have the opportunity to observe the student practise.

During one particular *jigsaw lesson,* I chose to do some knitting as a 'jigsaw' activity. My student thought I might have been 'dreaming' and would not have been aware that she had lost count of the number of octaves as she played a scale. So she decided to play a little game with me and kept going until she got to the end of the keyboard to test me out. Unaware of her motives at the time, I played along, allowing her to continue. She could not stop laughing when she reached the last note, as she waited curiously to find out if I had noticed; fortunately I had and we shared her amusement.

J also for JUMP PRACTICE

Play	Look	Jump	Wait	Play
Wait	Think			
	Prepare			

This is useful to help with fluency where there are jumps between notes or chords. Use *Zoom* to ensure that all notes and fingering are correct.

PLAY the note or notes before the jump.

WAIT for as long as necessary while you *look* at, *think* about and *prepare* for the notes to which you will be jumping.

Then JUMP and WAIT before playing the next note or notes.

Be sure that you are in the right place.

Then PLAY the note or notes.

Jump practice procedure:
PLAY - WAIT - look, think and prepare - JUMP - WAIT - PLAY

Repeat procedure.

On each repeat, gradually reduce the amount of time you WAIT until you can delete it altogether: PLAY JUMP PLAY. By now playing should be fluent.

K

K for KEEP FIT

Consider posture. Take breaks, stretch, shake and move around in between long sessions of practising. Look after yourself.

L

L for LESS IS MORE

Sometimes *less is more*. Sometimes you can achieve more by focusing and working successfully on one piece or one small aspect of the music.

L also for LOUD

Be reasonably sensitive to others around you when you are practising. Could you close the door, or practise scales or exercises at a better time?

M

M for MOTIVATION

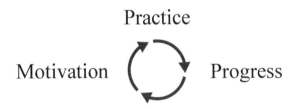

Practice

Motivation   Progress

What helps you with motivation to practise?

Students tend to practise most on the pieces they like the most. Is this a surprise?

When it comes to exam time or a performance, or reaching a specific goal, ask yourself: "What activities am I putting aside?"

Some students may benefit from reminders to practise and others do not need them. Here is my strategy for children who are not happy with the way their parents remind them to practise: secretly plan with your student for them to practise before their parents have a chance to remind them. Young students love secrets and surprising all concerned.

Text message reminders to practise and fill in the *Weekly Rhythm Record* (practice chart) have been requested by students and shown to work. Gentle reminders to practise from a family member or friend may help. Ask students what support they would like. Do they want to be reminded and by who? A 'no reminding me to practise week' works well in some cases.

A previous student of mine found it 'difficult to concentrate' and practise on her own. However, her parents continued to bring her for lessons. When it came to giving her the music for the Grade 1 piano pieces, she learned all three of them in just two weeks. Her mother informed me that she simply did not stop practising.

For motivation, we need to know we are making progress.

Do It Now!

N
N for a NINETY-SECOND PRACTICE

It was before school one morning when my daughter Natalie, then aged eight, only had a very short time to practise the piano; *ninety seconds* to be precise. Observing her, I was impressed that she had achieved more in that time than students sometimes do when they are practising for longer. It was quality work. Who can ever say, "I don't have time to practise?"

Quality not Quantity

O
O for OVER-PRACTICE

"Before I came to you for help with my musical performance I used to over-practice." Music college student

Performance nerves can change during a musical career. You may not be nervous at first. Then as you become aware of expectations, perhaps of the audience, you could become more nervous. You may then realise that the more you practise the less nervous you are.

The techniques in this book should help you to limit your use *over practice.*

P

P for OVERCOMING PROCRASTINATION

Here are some ways I overcame a practice block:

Planned – time of day to practise.
Determined – motivation check
Made the time

I can't practise because….
There are distractions, other things to do.
Most of the pieces were hard.
I did not like any of the pieces.
I can practise because….
There are no distractions.
I started with the pieces I already knew; it was fun.
I love the scales.

Just play something, anything.
Daily practice works, using the *Weekly Rhythm Record*
Encouragement to practise from a family member is appreciated.
I noticed good feelings once I started to practise. Often the more you play, the more you like what you are practising.

Manage yourself in time.

For help with self-sabotage on excuses for not practising, tap the Psychological Reversal PR spot (side of hand), see Appendix.

Talk to your teacher
Do It Now!

P also for PRACTISE with PATIENCE!

Q

Q for QUALITY NOT QUANTITY

If time is limited and you are going to do a little practice, do it well.

R

R for RECORD YOUR PRACTISING

Use this as a tool to improve your practising. How did you find it helpful? What did you or your teacher notice or learn from listening to these recordings?

R also for REPERTOIRE

Repertoire pieces need practising as well. Remove any mistakes that may have crept in, just like you would remove weeds when gardening. When those pieces have been learned well, they can be re-learned to performing standard in a relatively short amount of time.

R also for DIFFERENT RHYTHM PRACTICE

This will help fast passagework and scales to become more even and fluent. Single or double dotted rhythms can be used.

'Long - short - long'.
　　For the double dotted rhythm, make each long note very long and each short note very short.
　　Then reverse the rhythm to 'short - long - short' in a similar way. Then play evenly.

R also for REPEAT, REPEAT, REPEAT!

When the music is correct, *repeat* it again and again - correctly!
　　Once when I was learning a challenging piano accompaniment to a Brahms clarinet sonata, a musician friend said, "Go over and over it, really slowly." Did I need to be reminded? Yes, it is always good to be reminded of such things. Soon enough, slowly and surely the piece 'turned' into Brahms.

S

S for THE MUSICAL SECRET-ARY

 The *Musical Secretary* is a game that can help practising be effective and fun. There are two teams: the *reds* and the *greens*. The *reds* are for 'incorrect', where there is a mistake. The *greens* are for 'correct', where the music is played well.

Rules of the game:

Choose someone, such as a parent, to be the *musical secretary*. Most of the time when you are practising at home, that can be you, the performer or student. It can be your teacher during a lesson. This person will keep score, usually in writing. The *performer* is the one who decides which team scores, according to how the music is played.

Be specific - decide on *exactly* which part of the music you want to improve; for example, a single note, a phrase of music, or one of the *time savers*. This decision is most important for achieving success through this game. Any other mistake is ignored at this stage.[1]

When the music is played correctly, or well, the *musical secretary* will write the numeral ' one' in the G (green) column as if the green team have scored one 'goal' or point. If there is a mistake, a numeral 'one' in the R (red) colu mn will be written for the red team. The first to get to three will win. Of course, we want the green team to win; we want to get it 'right.' We often slow down automatically to ensure that we play the music correctly so as to score a point for the green team.

If the reds win, repeat the game, ensuring that the greens win the best of three games. The green team should always be the overall winners. Green for go, the new habit has been formed and you are ready to go on.

Lots of greens will indicate effective use of practice time. Lots of reds may well indicate frustration or boredom is growing; so do something different to get the greens winning: such as the *successipe* or *slow is fast progress*.

This game will encourage working on those *bits* that need extra practice, as well as improving the skill of *starting from different places* in the music.

---

[1] *Don't shoot the dog!* The new art of teaching and training by Karen Pryor published by Ringpress Books Ltd 2002

An aspiring concert pianist once told me that they love practising the piano, as every day they are achieving something through reaching many small and sometimes larger goals. In effect they were describing the *musical secretary,* which they do in their head.

It is most important to know when you are playing a *red* and here lies the challenge. The line in between the *red* and *green* columns can sometimes be like a fence to a student; sitting on that fence, you are unsure if you are playing the music 'right' or 'wrong'. You may not even realise you are playing a *red.* You may not even realise you are playing a *green.* This is where the teacher's guidance is necessary.

Remember when you are the *musical secretary* yourself and writing down your own scores, it does take a few more seconds to do this. It is effective and will be time well spent.

That the words *music secret* can be found within the *musical secret-ary* is more than a coincidence.

S also for SCALES

How do you or your students feel about scales?

For those who struggle to remember the notes and fingerings of the scales, help is at hand here and elsewhere in *Zoom88,* such as *time savers,* Chapter 15 *Cows Clefs and Key Notes,* or tapping the PR spot (side of hand) to help remove blocks - see Appendix.

Scales for piano:
Becoming fluent and knowing the notes in the right hand can often help the left hand as well. Use *Say Play* where needed to assist with note learning. *Scales Shapes* by Frederick Stocken, published by Chester Music 2010, may also be useful for some students.

Broken chords for piano:
Use *Say Play* for significant finger numbers as well as note names.

Practise by keeping all the notes down for each chord, until it is familiar. Then separate the chord into single notes, as written in the scale book.

Wind or string instruments:
Say play, time savers and *slow is fast progress* are very effective ways to practise the correct notes and fingerings, minimising

mistakes. Write out the note names of the scales if necessary. This will help with sequencing where needed.

Scales can be practised in different ways, such as varying the dynamics, rhythm, speed or articulation. This can help overcome boredom as well as improve technique.

Ensure *all* the required scales are practised enough to be known prior to entry for an exam. Once this has been achieved, as part of the preparation, include practising with a 'mock examiner' giving instructions as might be used during an exam. This helps eliminate any unnecessary confusion.

During the process of writing this book, I have changed the way in which I prepare candidates for playing their scales for ABRSM exams: I stopped 'jumping' and follow the syllabus order, missing out the word *scale* or *arpeggio* when asking a number of these in succession.

Student comments:
'I like the scales because they are interesting and I find I can get on with practising them. They completely take me away from everything else in life. After you have helped me with fingering they are easier now.'

S also for SPEED PRACTICE
Start the passage you are practising as slowly as you possibly can. Each time you repeat it, *gradually increase the speed* until it is *too fast* for you to play it properly. Then *gradually decrease the speed*, until you are back to playing *very slowly*.

S also for THE SUCCESSIPE of *how* to practise music.

The recipe for successful music practice

My student Alec suggested the word *successipe* to me when I presented him with a 'recipe for success' for his practising during one of his piano lessons. It is now a successful method of *how* to practise and helps with making the best use of practice time.

Students may say, "I've practised." It is usually obvious when they have not used the *successipe*. In fact, I have even gone as far as saying "use the successipe" rather than suggesting a student should go home and practise.

Beware of over confidence; "I didn't think I needed to use the *successipe*," or "I didn't think I needed to use all of it." Some players think they can get away with it; professionals know they cannot. Be professional in your attitude and approach.

Method and the seven main 'ingredients' of the successipe:

Preparation: ☺ Managing your state

1. Say play
2. Zoom
3. Slowly
4. Time Savers (TS)
5. Bits
6. Hands Separately (HS)
7. Basic Practice (BP)

Keep track: The Weekly Rhythm Record (WRR)

The order is important. From left to right on the *successipe chart*, see Appendix.

Each part of the *successipe* can be used individually and can make a lesson on its own.

Use ALL of the *successipe*, or as much as is appropriate, for the aspect or section of music you are practising. It can help with minimising mistakes.

Preparation: ☺ Managing your state

What state are you in right now? How focused and ready to practise are you? Use Thought Field Therapy TFT tapping (see Appendix) or other appropriate technique if and when needed.

1. SAY PLAY

SAY the *letter* name (ABC...) of the note aloud, including any sharps, flats or naturals, and then PLAY it.

Pianists: start with hands separately.

Say Play is what musicians silently use when learning music. It is a process that has become automatic.

The student is blissfully unaware that *Say Play* is actually slowing them down so they can play accurately.

Students often seem to do the reverse - 'play say'. This can be quickly turned into *Say Play*.

Adaptations and variations:
A variation for piano students who are just beginning to play hands together, or wherever it is needed:
SAY aloud
*   which *hand* the note is to be played with
*   the *letter name* of the note
*   which *finger number* is to be used and then
PLAY it.

For wind players use 'SAY FINGER' in a similar way:
SAY the letter name of the note, and then FINGER it before playing.

For string players, to help with intonation and finding the correct finger position, use 'SING PLAY':
SING and PLAY the note before the one you want to correct.
Then SING the note you want to correct. Then PLAY this note.

Although he did not call it *sing play*, cellist Raphael Wallfisch effectively taught me this technique when I used to have a habit of playing a note on my cello and then sliding around in an attempt to find the correct pitch.

2. ZOOM! - aka The 88 model lesson
(Oh, so that is where she got the title of this book from.)

1. ZOOM
2. SLOWLY
3. Hands Separately (for pianists)

It is 'ok' to make a mistake as long as you notice it.
Use the *musical secretary*

TIME SAVERS - observe the *time savers*
COUNT ALOUD - count the beats of the rhythm aloud

I originally called this *the 88 model lesson.* My piano student - my mother Josie - was 88 and preparing for her Grade 3 piano exam when she had her stroke (see Chapter 32). We did not know whether she would survive. At this time, I had become fascinated as to how many of my other piano students, who could see their music more clearly than my mother, were making and not noticing some of their mistakes when practising or performing. I decided to break down just how Josie achieved what she did in her piano playing. In tribute to and in recognition of her being my 'model student', I developed *the 88 model lesson.* It is now called *Zoom*, to make it easier to remember the content.

The *88 model lesson*, as it was called, became such an important lesson in my teaching, that as a reminder to my students I placed an 88 'card' on the piano (see photo). It was originally a birthday 'card,' made by my daughter Natalie for her Grandpa Sam when he was aged eighty-eight.

I begin this lesson by telling the story of how Josie needed to use a *magnifying glass* to be able to see the music clearly. I ask the student to *zoom* in and take a close look at the music, sometimes looking to the left, to the beginning of the bar or stave, in order to observe clefs, key signatures or accidentals. *Zoom* is like taking a photograph or a musical sound picture of the musical notation and performance directions.

I am sure you will enjoy this lesson as much as I do. It gives the student *permission to make mistakes*, which they could have become anxious about in their efforts to avoid them. It is a great way to relax the student and at the same time help them to observe the music more closely.

3. SLOWLY – simply focus on playing slowly.
See Chapter 9 *Slow is fast progress* for further tips and ideas on how to help you or your students to play slower.

4. TIME SAVERS

Ask yourself: Did I do the **Time Savers**?

Time Savers, as I call them, are the various markings of visual reminders or 'alerts' which musicians write onto the music. They are used to assist with those 'musical adjustments', to speed up learning, enable accurate practice and achieve a more authentic, effective or secure performance.

If there are no hand-written *time savers*, use any of the printed performance directions in the music, such as dynamics and articulation, in a similar way.

Just after you have played the music that has the *time saver* on it, ask the question: *"Did I do the time saver?"* In this way, time is being saved in the lesson as it is helping you to reduce or eliminate those unnecessary mistakes. It can also help you to save time in your practising at home and minimise frustration.

I suggest *time savers* be used with some degree of discretion for students. I have seen music where a teacher has overused the *time savers*, writing in finger numbers or letter names for every note; or a flat sign before every note B and in another piece, a sharp sign for every note F, where in both cases there was a key signature. This approach can lead to difficulties in reading and performing music in the future. See Chapter 15 *Cov vs, Clefs and Key Notes*.

I have also accompanied students who were having difficulty with some rhythms. They had learned the music simply by ear, by copying the sounds. When I looked at their music, no *time savers* for counting had been included; I then wrote them in, with the students assisting where they could, enabling a much-improved performance.

It is important to make sure students appreciate and know, simply by asking them, exactly what the *time savers* are and what each represents. They are not just 'teacher scribbles'!

I write my *time savers* in pencil so students can enjoy seeing their progress as they choose and decide which ones they want to *keep* and which they are happy to *delete* and have erased.

When students write in or adjust *time savers* on their own music, it will assist their practising and encourage them to think for themselves. There is no need to remove all *time savers* for you or for exam purposes.

When you are practising, work on each *time saver,* one at a time.

THE THINKING CIRCLE

One of the most common *time savers* is what I call the *thinking circle.* It is like an 'awareness circle'. These are the circles written around certain notes or bars where reminders are needed, or mistakes have occurred. They invite you, during practice and the learning stages, to STOP and have a 'THINK' about the notes before you play them to ensure that they will be played correctly. I have even drawn traffic lights with 'red' showing, to help those who need an extra reminder to stop and think.

Use *Say Play* for the *thinking circles* where appropriate.

The *thinking circle* helps you to have time to *be sure.*

Tapping the PR spot (side of hand) can be used to increase concentration or correct reversals.

THE TIME SAVERS PRACTICE

Just practise all the *time savers.*

It will help with fluency.

Student comment:

"I may as well learn it correctly in the first place - it'll save me a lot of time later."

5. BITS – Practise only the part that needs to be improved, in bite-sized chunks. Even when a piece of music is well learned, still remember to *start in different places* and end a few bars later.

6. HANDS SEPARATELY for pianists. Even when a piece is well learned, it is so important to still practise *hands separately,* particularly the more challenging passages. Mistakes can all too easily creep in if this is not done. My piano teacher Eva used to say, "Never underestimate the left hand."

7. BASIC PRACTICE

Practice *slowly* in short sections, for example two to four bars.

Play the passage three times *correctly*. If there are mistakes, use *the musical secretary*.

For pianists:
Right Hand – three times
Left Hand – three times
Hands Together – three times

Keep track: The Weekly Rhythm Record (WRR)

See Appendix

I began using this particular chart - because of the success of the *Compound Effect*[2] – to track practising for myself and for my music students during our '*Musical Olympics*' in 2012, the year in which the Olympics were held in London. It encourages *daily* practice, getting into a 'rhythm' – a word so essential to music and life.

While any practice chart is useful, I find it helpful to have the same one for most of my students, even if they use it in an individual way. The chart is for both the teacher and the student. It will assist in giving the teacher an immediate idea of how much practice has been done since the last lesson. It will take you from 'I think I practised' to 'I know I practised'. It can help with overcoming procrastination and with motivation to practise. Consider, how is it useful to you? What does it help with?

The challenge is to get students to complete the *Weekly Rhythm Record* and bring it along to their lessons. To avoid the inevitable, "I did it; it's at home", ensure students secure it into, for example, their tutor book, scale book or notebook.

The chart can be completed to record and track the actual amount of time spent daily and weekly to nearest five minutes. *Practice ticks* can also be useful for getting into the 'practising habit'.

One needs to *make* the time to practise, even if that means getting up earlier in the morning. Find a regular time of day to practise if that works well for you.

---

[2] *The Compound Effect* Multiplying your success one simple step at a time by Darren Hardy published by SUCCESS Books 2010

When do you practise? One student told me he used to practise 'in his spare moments - as and when'. The *Weekly Rhythm Record* changed this. Patterns can be noticed. Does your student practise as soon as possible after their lesson, or for example, is there a valid reason that they do not practise on a particular day?

TEN MINUTES MORE.

A task, such as *ten minutes more*, can be set to raise amounts of daily practice or practice done over a week. A gradual increase like this can help prevent injury.

A number of my students have gone on to use the *Weekly Rhythm Record* to help with various other aspects in their life, from homework to press-ups.

* * *

When the music is learned, a slimmed down version of the *successipe* can be used.

"Is practising about sticking to the *successipe*?" one of my students asked.

"Is there a place for '*successipe* music teachers'?" my student Alec asked.

Once you have put the *successipe* into practice, do let the author know what you think about this or how the *successipe* has worked for you or your students'.

T

T for TALLY PRACTICE

This is a 'play until it is easy' approach. I remember my piano teacher Eva writing 'x 100' next to one bar of music. There are certain parts of the music, some *bits*, that just need more practice than as outlined in *the musical secretary*; use *Tally Practice* to track this, as it can be easy to think you have practised more than you actually have.

T also for THE TIMER LESSON

Time exactly how long it takes to play a piece of music accurately, however slow it is, however long it takes. The following week, time it again in a similar way. This is a good measure of progress and can be very motivating.

U

U for ASK USEFUL QUESTIONS

When you are practising ask yourself useful questions such as:
What do I need to do in this practice session?
Was that better?
Could it be even better?
What do I need to do to get it better?
What could I do to get it even better?
How could I improve it?
What is hard?
What is easier?
What do you notice about your practising?
How do you feel about practising?
What are your practising challenges?

Discuss these with your teacher.

V

V for VIRTUOSO

How does a virtuoso practise? Ask someone you regard as an excellent player and ask how he or she practises?

W

W for WARM UP and WARM DOWN

Warm up your body (as well as your wind instrument or voice) before starting to practise, such as some simple stretches, shoulder shrugs or breathing exercises. See Appendix *Look after your voice*. After a longer practice, warm down your body as above.

X

X for 'X-Ray Eyes' are needed for learning and practising music.

Y

Y for WHY

W*hy* are you practising? Are you working towards a particular performance? What do you want to achieve as you practise?

Z

Z for ZOOM!

* * *

TIPS ON PRACTISING
FROM SOME OF ROSEMARY'S STUDENTS

'*Want* to practise rather than be nagged to practise'

'Enjoy the music that you are playing'

'Practise when you are bored or when you are *gently* reminded'

'Concentrate'

'Regular practice'

'*Wanting* to do an exam'

'Quality not Quantity - as Rosemary would say'

'Go over things, correctly played, *lots* of times'

'Check on yourself …maybe you need to practise *more* '

'Build up practice is useful'

'Use a timer'

'A kitchen timer that buzzes, for example after quarter of an hour's practice.'

'If you do not have much time, set a buzzer for ten minutes and then carry on if you want for longer.'

'Really *look* at the music'

'Have someone with you who will just *listen* and know that you will correct yourself if you are wrong.'

'Think for a minute and correct *yourself*'

'Put your own marks on the music for visual reminders, for example circle the notes.'

'The *ninety second practice*, with concentration and slowly.'

'Be determined'

'DO IT NOW!'

'Rosemary says if you go over the music more you will like it more.'

* * *

The most interesting results can occur when *no* practice has been done in-between performances of a piece.
See Appendix *Brief notes of Music Students helped by Thought Field Therapy (TFT)*.

* * *

Positive practice will promote positive performance. In the next chapter you can get some more help with what causes one of the biggest fears of a performance going well.

Schoolgirl's love of music

ROSEMARY Woolfe, a 14-year-old schoolgirl from Aylestone Avenue, Brondesbury, manages to combine her academic studies with a love of music.

During the day she is hard at work learning history, biology, maths, music, geography, English, French and Hebrew and in her leisure time in the evening she plays her recorder, cello and piano.

"I am now entering my fourth year at the Jewish Free School in Camden Road where I am fortunate enough to have a very able music teacher who gives me every encouragement to make my career in music.

"When I leave school I want to go to college and train to become a music teacher."

Whenever she gets the chance, Rosemary plays at concerts for crippled folk or at homes for the blind.

At the weekends she seizes any opportunity to attend live concerts to pick up a few hints from professional musicians.

The daughter of a furniture manufacturer, she had her ambition realised this year when she won a gold medal in the solo recorder section of the 1970 Brent Music and Dance Festival.

Her success at this major competitive event has prompted her to enter again next year — only this time she will be trying her luck on the piano.

Staff Photo No. C/6873/A

● Rosemary Woolfe

Willesden & Brent Chronicle; Kilburn Times. October 2nd, 1970.

Willesden & Brent Chronicle and Kilburn Times newspapers. 2nd October 1970

With Judy (right) - Safari Park, Doune Castle, Scotland 1974

Cello with Candy - one musical dog.

Tapping with my mother, Josie Woolf.
Photo published in Health Quarterly Winter 2008

Josie Woolf doing her 'armchair practice' 2015

Entertaining at Hill House Care Home for Josie's Life After Stroke Award 2015

88 birthday 'card' design by Natalie Wiseman

Chapter 12
Mistaikes and expectations

"My piano lesson was fair. I wish I didn't make some of the mistakes I do." J (quote from my journal)

'There are no mistakes or failures, only lessons.' - Denis Waitley

Mistaikes, like the misspelling of this word, can make you feel uncomfortable. They can occur in practice and performance. If you find you are making too many, use the ideas suggested here to help you. They will enhance your ability to learn and improve your performance.

Student performers conversations can go rather like this:

"Why am I playing a C#?"
"Well at least I noticed it."
"Can I play it again?"
"Will I get it right this time?"
"There it goes again."
"I wonder why it's gone wrong?"
"Normally I go so fast, I don't know I've made a mistake."
"My brain knows where my hands should be going, but my fingers are going for a different scale."

How familiar do the following phrases sound to you?
"I always make that mistake."
"I always get muddled up with the left hand fingering here."
"I keep getting this bit wrong."

When my students used to say these words, it intrigued me. Clearly they had been practising these mistakes since their last lesson. I just did not know how to help them. It was well before I had come to learn any of the therapeutic techniques I have written about in *Zoom88*. However, I told them some stories that in effect became the beginning of the lesson you are about to read, on dealing with and gaining greater understanding about mistakes.

The tomato story

As a music teacher, allowing my students to feel that in the 'safe space' of my music room they can make mistakes and then learn from them is very important, as in this *Tomato Story*:

My neighbour Len found it most frustrating to watch me struggling to grow a few tomatoes, as he could see I spent much time pinching out the leaves incorrectly. Meanwhile, next door, Len was spending a similar amount of time and producing many pounds of tomatoes.

Fortunately, one day Len had the courage to come and offer me a 'lesson' on how to pinch out those leaves correctly. He said it was quite OK to make a mistake once. It was a joy to discover that with the same amount of effort, I was able to yield *many* more tomatoes.

In the days that followed, I imagined that Len used to watch me from his window next door, just checking to make sure I never made the same mistake again.

The ironing story

 'Iron it out!' - Get rid of those mistakes quickly!

Have you ever done any ironing or watched someone doing so? It can happen so easily; by mistake you can find yourself momentarily losing concentration and ironing a crease in the wrong place. When this happens it requires a lot more work to remove the crease. So it is with mistakes on our musical instrument. A lot of concentration is required to notice our mistakes so that if we make one, at least we will not repeat it and 'iron it in.'

For some students who had become really good at making and then practising their mistakes,[1] I would write the following words in their notebooks:

'WhatEVER you practise you get BETTER at.'

What we always do, we get good at.

Take care to ensure that your notes are correct. As muscle memory sets in, you will learn them quickly.

* * *

Although slips and mistakes can be an annoying part of learning, they are part of the process. Still, I believe they can be reduced or handled better; practice time can be saved and difficulties or frustration during performance minimised.

So what are the causes of musical mistakes? They may fall into at least one of these categories:

"It's only because I am unsure about something."
"It was just today."
"I was unaware and did not know I made them."
"I was aware - I keep making that mistake at home."
"I have not been practising, or practising effectively."

A for ANXIETY

Some of the most common causes of mistakes are performance anxiety or the fear of making mistakes. This chapter and *Zoom88* will give you many resources for calmer, more expressive and enjoyable music making.

---

[1] See Appendix Brief notes on Music Students helped by Thought Field Therapy TFT

B for BOXING GLOVE

In my music room there is a very special boxing glove, which is signed by Paul McGee:

'S.U.M.O.!

Paul The Sumo Guy.'[2]

A piano student came to me as her parents were concerned about her progress and together with her teacher they were unsure how and when she would be able to take her first grade. She was having difficulties reading music. She demonstrated how she would slap her knee when she was annoyed with herself for making mistakes.

Can you remember feeling this way about some of your seemingly inexplicable mistakes and hitting yourself or taking out your frustrations on your instrument, like some sportsmen do on their equipment?

Whilst there are a small number of students who may laugh at their mistakes, many naturally get frustrated.

Usually those students who appear to 'beat themselves up' want, or expect, accurate and instant results. It may be that they are comparing themselves to other people who have succeeded. Some have an internal dialogue of negative thoughts, causing tension; with others it may show physically, by them literally hitting themselves when they make mistakes.

Put that *boxing glove* down!

Student comment:

"The *boxing glove* is useful for me and my brother. I can picture it in my head. It reminds you to stop getting annoyed."

F for FINGERING

Mistakes often occur due to incorrect, unsuitable or inconsistent fingering. Occasionally they can be useful, such as when you discover a better fingering. Above all, fingering needs to be consistent for accuracy.

---

[2] S.U.M.O. (Shut Up, Move On or Stop, Understand, Move On) by Paul McGee. First published 2005. Latest edition 2015

L for LEARNING

Take your time when learning music. See those stumbles as stepping-stones.

Mistakes are an opportunity to learn; you have just not found the correct way to play or perform the music yet - you certainly need to do something different.

If something is going wrong, you are not doing something right – Zoom88!

M for MAKE SOME MISTAKES

There can be an over concern about mistakes made or the possibility of making them, usually at the expense of making expressive and enjoyable music.

Sometimes the harder you try not to make mistakes the more you will make them. So now, give yourself permission to make some mistakes, ZOOM88! Say, "it's OK if I make a mistake," or "it's alright if I am not sure about something yet."

One of my piano students calls my music room 'the rehearsal room' and another imagines it is padded so no-one else can hear. You are free to experiment with the sounds you make. They can be edited as in a recording studio.

Mistakes guide you and lack of them can show you signs of progress.

When practising...

Once you are aware you have made a mistake, STOP and sort it out or ask for help. 'Delete' it and 'forget' it as quickly as possible and use *The Musical Secretary*!

When performing...

'It's good to make mistakes so we can practise covering them up. The show must go on.' Dame Fanny Waterman

I am giving a mini master class and my student Carla is about to play a piece she is still working on. She says, "I think I am going to make a mistake." We change the expectations so she realises that in this performance, mistakes are acceptable as she is still at the 'learning stage'. Carla plays her best and any mistakes do not hinder her overall performance.

Once all the practice and preparations have been done, expressive and emotional communication are more important than technical perfection when performing.

O for OVER CONFIDENCE

Sometimes mistakes can occur due to over-confidence. "I did not think I needed to use (all of) the *successipe* or do it in the right order." The consequences of not doing the *successipe* and not learning the right notes straight away can mean that the music sounds strange when it is played correctly.

R for REVERSALS

Since being introduced to TFT tapping in 2001, I have collected numerous examples (over 60) of mistakes made due to 'reversals' – learning blocks due to psychological reversal (PR)[3]. Many of these were corrected with the appropriate treatment, such as tapping the PR spot (side of hand). It showed me that clef, right or left and directional confusions were far more prevalent than I had ever realised. Moreover, I learned about possible causes and what could be done about them. Consequently, I was able to distinguish student difficulties resulting from this, as opposed to a lack of practice.

Some mistakes are far from 'accidental'. I would ask the student how they worked out the letter names of the notes and they would tell me their methods, which appeared quite logical.

These kinds of mistakes, where they have 'recomposed' the piece, are not recognised by students and they do not know how to correct them. They may not even realise that, after TFT tapping, their fingers will go to different (and correct) notes. The student's intention is the same, so after TFT - when the performance is clearly better - they can be somewhat bemused as to how this has happened. It can be a strange and pleasurable experience.

---

[3] PR is a state characterised by a reversal of concepts and self-sabotaging behaviour. There are several treatments, the simplest involving tapping the PR spot on the side of the hand. See *Tapping the Healer Within* and Appendix for further details.

Anna's reversed version, her re-composition, of Yankee Doodle:

CCBAGAB, CCDECB, CCBAGABC, DFEDCC

In this case, after simply tapping the PR spot (side of hand) and under nose (UN), Anna was able to play the correct and original version of Yankee Doodle:

CCDECED, CCDECB, CCDEFEDC, BGABCC

Some students learn to recognise their own reversals in practice or performance and then find that they can correct them themselves.

Problems with reversals during practice can sometimes explain why something corrected in one lesson can again be wrong the following week.

S for SORRY

Sorry

‖

Thank you for
noticing that

‖⫟‖

Imagine a tennis player apologising for every mistake they make.

Where students over-use the word 'sorry' as they apologise for their mistakes, I encourage them to replace it by saying aloud, "Thank you for noticing that." If they have not noticed the mistake and I have, they can say, "Thank you for noticing that Rosemary." Later these words may be internalised. This is a very effective way to reduce or even replace the word 'sorry', giving them an appreciation of their important ability to be aware of and learn from mistakes. A secondary benefit can be that in relaxing more about making mistakes, they make less of them.

I may then ask, 'What did you notice?'

This can lead to useful discussion about what mistakes have been noticed and what improvements can be made.

Say to yourself, "It is good to notice my mistakes."

T for TFT TAPPING

One of my young students has performed very well in previous concerts. It is the day before her first piano exam - for which she went on to achieve a merit. She has that common mixture of excitement and nervousness. In her third piece there are a number of mistakes causing some inaccuracies. There is no more time to correct them and by now she has become quite upset with her performance. After a short TFT tapping sequence for simple trauma, there is total accuracy.

It can be worth checking to find out if there are any significant causes of mistakes due to distraction. One of my students was making an unusual amount of errors in her cello lesson. I discovered she was nervous about her performance as she was singing in a concert that night and had concerns about 'getting it right'.

Identify the Thought Field for exactly what is bothering you and tap the appropriate sequence for it.

TFT can be used to treat frustration, a fear of making mistakes and anxiety about memory lapses (see Appendix).

TIPS

For those inexplicable mistakes, sometimes it is helpful to simply breathe deeply or stop and come back to the music later.

Add any errors you make to the big pot of mistakes that are made by professional musicians. All musicians make mistakes. We are all human!

Here are some of the useful lessons and chapters in *Zoom88* which can help with mistakes:

B for Be Sure
D for The Musical Detective
E for Expectations
G for Goalposts – We both move them
L for Learning; The A----B line
M for MUF – The musical triangle of communication
S for The Successipe
Also:
Cows Clefs and Key Notes
Improve your practising
Slow is fast progress

Here are some typical PRACTICE TRAPS or REALITY GAPS:

- Not realising that you have made a mistake, finishing the piece and then carrying on.
- Playing a piece of music through only once and thinking you have practised. This is a 'mistake' in itself.
- Practising a mistake. Our fingers learn fast, whether it is right or wrong.

When performing, it can be hard for perfectionist students not to correct themselves. They may feel an uncomfortable sense of lack of control: "I get lost. I don't know where I am. I need to find…"

Now it is time to perform and to stop thinking about getting the 'right notes'.

Chapter 13
Improve your performance

Performing music can be demanding. It can also be an intensely enjoyable and satisfying experience. Music is even more rewarding if you share it. It is a way to express yourself and reveal your deepest emotions and is a good and healthy thing to do. It can increase self-confidence, build self-esteem and give much pleasure to yourself and others.

Performance requires practice. Music exams can be useful for this, as well as providing motivation. *Make an audience, mini master classes* or *overlap lessons* give more frequent opportunities for practice. Performance skills and anxiety about playing or singing can be covered in these sessions.

So how can we improve our musical performance (or that of our students) assuming that all the necessary practising has now been done? To perform at your best you will need relaxed concentration, be calm and focused, confident and in control. Part three of this book highlights selected cases that demonstrate this.

Reducing performance anxiety, also known as 'stage fright', is possible with natural, non-invasive and effective techniques that do not involve artificial stimulants, for example alcohol or beta-blocker drugs. There are healthier ways, which you will be learning more about in this book.

Tips and experiences of other performers

"I played it better at home."

How often do you hear these words from your students? They remind me of a past piano student. Together, during one particular lesson, we explored this phenomenon to rule out performance anxiety and I even offered to leave the room, just in case I was the cause. The following week she said, "It's not you, it's me. I just needed to practise more."

For another performer, who really has prepared effectively, yet is still anxious, an appropriate state management technique can be used. For some, that could simply be talking about their performance concerns or unrelated subjects that distract or calm them.

TFT tapping: for visualising peak performance, anxiety, frustrations or traumas (see Appendix).

On Performing

Think how you want the music to sound before you play it.

Isaac Stern, one of the greatest violinists of the 20th century, described his style of playing as like the "*natural rise and fall of the human voice. . . . You sing in your head and you play what you hear.*"

Be musical – SING
Instrumentalists, play your music as if you were singing it.
Consider where would you breathe?

What is the title of your piece?
What is its style and character?
Who is the composer?
What do these mean to you regarding the piece?

Do you like it? Why have you chosen to perform it?
Focus on and enjoy the music; mean what you 'say' and 'say' what you mean.
Enjoy the creative experience of 'making it your own.'

Above all, when you are performing - KEEP GOING!

A Mini Masterclass

Carla is preparing for her Grade 2 piano exam in a few months. At the end of a lesson I invite her and Gina, a prep test level student, to perform to each other as part of a mini masterclass. This is to develop their performance skills and show both students and parents how I teach different levels.

Gina says, "You can get rid of nerves." Today she tells us she feels anxious and excited. On a scale of one to ten with ten being the most troubled and one being the most calm, she is a six. I invite her father and Carla's mother in and she is now an eight.

Knowing that she is well prepared, I ask Gina whether she would like to tap a TFT sequence to reduce anxiety, or just play. On this occasion she chooses to play. I am sure that having the choice to calm any nerves at this moment has empowered her. Her internal thoughts in those moments, she tells me afterwards, were, "I can do it. I have done this before." Her nerves quickly disappear once she starts playing. Thinking positively and being well prepared, Gina performs her piece well.

Carla meanwhile was quite nervous for a different reason. She is unprepared, as she is still working on and improving her piece. She is worried that she is going to make mistakes. I reassure her that it will be OK for her to make mistakes. With this permission, Carla presents a flowing performance with minimal slips. Most important is the positive feeling she has afterwards.

Parents can get nervous before their child's performance, even when their child does not. Alma Deutscher, the young child prodigy, says she is "only excited and not nervous" before a performance. However, her mother gets nervous for her. This is a common situation in an exam waiting room. I have been known to guide parents through the TFT tapping sequence for anxiety prior to their child's exam.

Simon is preparing for his Grade 1 clarinet exam and looking forward to it. "Being above the grade makes me feel more relaxed about it." He went on to pass with distinction.

Aim for a high performance 'standard', so your Performance becomes your Perform Ace!

Chapter 14
Enjoy sight-reading

Some difficulties in sight-reading are due to reading music too slowly, perhaps from learning it originally by using mnemonics, or the over-use of *time savers* - music marked, for example, with every single note named or fingered.

Another common cause is the natural desire to be 'perfect' and correct mistakes, or repeat notes - quite the opposite of what is required to be a good sight-reader.

A significant problem for some students is *reversals*. These can occur in sight-reading due to minimal practice and insufficient time for self-correction (see Appendix *Brief notes and music students helped by TFT*).

I was once asked to assist a piano teacher who needed help with their Grade 5 piano student who could play his pieces well, yet was having difficulties with the sight-reading. I quickly discovered he was reading music from right to left, instead of left to right! He was quite amazed when this was pointed out and explained it later to his parents with great excitement. Other *reversals*, related to pitch, were also evident. Tapping the PR spot (side of hand) corrected these problems immediately.

If there are frequent *reversals*, do some TFT tapping, such as the PR spot (side of hand) or the collar bone breathing, to speed up music reading and make it easier (see Appendix).

Advantages of being a good sight-reader
It will help you to learn new pieces more quickly. You can have more enjoyment and fun making music on your own as well as with others. It is a great asset if you are an accompanist.

Sight-reading can be fun.
If you think you are 'bad at sight-reading', follow the suggestions in this chapter and build up confidence; choose music you can play *easily* until you can say, "I love sight-reading; it's *fun*!" or "I feel relaxed about sight-reading."

Some practising ideas

Apart from sight-reading tests, play some easy pieces that you can learn quickly.

Play just the beginnings of pieces - as if you are doing this to choose which one you would like to learn.

The best sight-readers are exceptionally good at *reading ahead*.

Have your teacher cover up the music of each bar as you play it, moving steadily along, to ensure you are reading *ahead* and that you *keep going*.

A *think ahead* mindset is very useful.

Speed up your music reading by keeping your *eyes on the music* as much as possible, or using the *Key Notes* system if needed.

The sight-reading performance

Tap the PR spot (side of hand) if you are prone to *reversals* and want to speed up your reading or perform your best.

Consider the title of the piece and performance directions such as tempo, character, style and mood.

Look carefully at the *key signature*. Know which sharps, flats or accidentals are required. If necessary, at the beginning of each bar keep repeating the words 'key signature' as you play, until the key is well established.

Observe the *time signature* and work out how you will be counting the music.

Scan all of the music for dynamics, performance instructions, or any other special features.

In an exam, during the preparation time, you can practise the sight-reading test *aloud*.

Piano and string players - get your hands in the correct position before playing the first notes.

Relax into the music as much as you can.

As you play, remember to *count*.

Observe the *dynamics* - they will help you to express the mood and give the piece shape and meaning.

Keep going! It is essential to do this during the performance. Recover quickly and do your best to accept and move on from any mistakes made. Make this a 'rule' and develop a 'keep going' habit.

Play or sing at a suitable *tempo* where you can manage to keep going.

Play or sing the *notes* as accurately as you can.

The *Sight-Reading Record Chart* suggests various criteria in order of priorities, left to right (see Appendix).

With knowledge and understanding your sight-reading will improve. Whilst there are many ways of achieving this, as with other aspects of musical performance, lots of effective and efficient practice helps.

Chapter 15
Cows, Clefs and Key Notes

Do you read music?

How do you read music?

How did you learn to read music?

Did you just get used to it, note by note, by doing it over and over, again and again, as with learning many new things? Or was there a system used by your teacher to assist you?

The traditional way of learning to read musical notation is the use of mnemonics, such as the popular 'All Cows Eat Grass' or similar phrases. Sometimes a musical ladder of successive notes on the stave is also printed in tutor books. The idea is to facilitate the learning of musical notes on the lines and spaces of the stave in the clef, or clefs, used for that instrument.

One day, many years after he had passed his Grade 4 piano and Grade 8 trumpet exams, I noticed my son David looking up some notes on a music reading device I had. He was actually searching for the bass clef notes of the piano so he could learn some new music by himself.

At that moment I realised that (as his piano teacher) I had not taught him to read the bass clef effectively; I had been unaware he had difficulties in this area at the time.

When I was a teenager, a close friend gave me a copy of the Bach Cello Suites as she had decided to stop learning the cello. When I looked at the Prelude in G major that she had learned, I noticed that every note had a fingering on it. She told me that this was because she was unable to read music. Since then I have discovered that many people who could not read music have had their music marked in a similar way, with over-use of these *time savers,* usually by their teachers.

Anthony, an adult student, came to me for piano lessons after a break of many years from playing this instrument. He was very musical and played with lots of expression, including his favourite warm up piece, Mozart's *Alla Turca*. Yet he was seemingly 'stuck' with working out ALL the notes using the mnemonic 'All Cows Eat Grass', in his case, for both bass AND treble clefs. It caused him to wonder if he had musical dyslexia.

It was experiences like these that led me to search for other speedier and more effective ways of teaching music reading. Over time this developed into what I call the 'Key Notes' - an efficient method of anchoring musical notes into the mind.

I noticed that my beginners on piano became less reliant on using the finger numbers to read music. It is for this reason that I like to use *Me and My Piano* Parts 1 and 2 by Dame Fanny Waterman and Marion Harewood, as it has less fingering in than some other tutor books.

The *key notes* are best described in a testimonial by one of my piano students, which explains the method she has learned through me.

"Since Rosemary started teaching me, we soon realised that I was quite unstable with my music reading. Ever since I started learning piano, I always struggled in that aspect of learning to play the piano. Now, many years on, I still have that problem.

However, when Rosemary realised I was struggling, she helped me to overcome this problem and she taught me one of her methods which has helped me a lot with my music reading.

This method is known as 'key notes'. It's simply remembering where three notes are on a stave in each hand and when coming across a note, you would think to yourself, "Is it a key note?"

If it's not, ask yourself which key note it is nearest to and then work out the note from there.

The phrase, 'Caring Freddie Cares' is used to remember the three notes, C, F, C.

Now middle C, I have always known, so that's the starting C.

Then F in the right hand is on the first space and in the left hand on the line in between the two dots of the bass clef.

The other C is three spaces up in the treble clef and three spaces down in the bass clef.

Now, when I read music, as long as I remember to use this new method, I find it so much easier to read my notes. I don't feel that it's such a struggle anymore and I feel confident to look at any piece of music and attempt playing it."

The Rosemary Wiseman 'Key Notes' Method

'Key Notes'

The way into reading music

Caring Freddie Cares

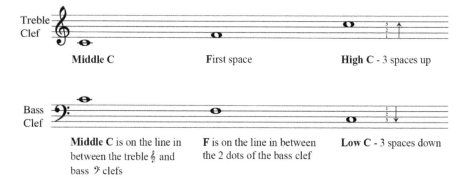

The Key Note Questions - to work out any note:

1. Is it a key note? (If the answer is 'no', go to no. 2)

2. Which key note is nearest?

3. ↑↓ From this key note to the note you want to name, do you need to go up or down?

4. ⟋ How many steps do you need to go to get to the note you want to name?

The Musical Ladder

Locate and play the *key notes* at the correct pitch on your musical instrument.

The *key notes* can be adapted for different instruments, keeping to the notes CFC - **C**aring **F**reddie **C**ares. Here are some examples:

For cello players: use the lowest note on cello - C on the ledger line below the bass clef stave - as a *key note*.

For flute players: use the top line of the treble clef, F and CFC on the ledger lines above, for what I call the 'advanced key notes'.

Learning the Key Notes

Work on one thing at a time, one note at a time, as you are beginning to use that note in your music. For learning the *key notes,* use repetition, including saying aloud the 'reasons'. For example: 'high C is 3 spaces up.' Write them out daily on manuscript paper or use visualisation, until you know them. The time spent learning them will be time well spent. Gradually you will become free of needing to use the *key notes*.

One of my students was finding it hard to read some music. We used the *key notes* to help her. "What is the point of the *key notes*?" she asked. I replied, "They are the 'key', like the way to open a door; think of them as the way into reading music. From these notes you can learn to read any other note."

If you are having difficulty reading music - use the *key notes*!

Music Reading

If you are stuck with the 'cows', put them out to 'grass' and stop using them. You will find the *key notes* will help you speed up your reading and give you freedom from having to use mnemonics or rhymes.

B for BE SURE

There is NO guessing in the reading of music.

Using the *key notes* method ask yourself HOW you 'KNOW SO.'
For example: How do you know that that note is an F?

Concentrate and work out the music using the *key notes* or ask for help with them. Then the music can be played correctly.

Are you stuck with the 'cows' or clefs?

How do you know if you are stuck with the 'cows'?

Here are some other cases of students who have, unwittingly, had to work far too hard to read music. Although they are all piano players, I have come across similar problems with 'single line' instrumentalists as well.

James was learning Grade 3 theory with me while he was working towards his Grade 5 violin and piano. He had incorrectly placed two sharps for the key signature of B minor on the stave on a theory practice paper. On asking him to explain this I discovered that he was stuck with the 'treble clef' and unable to read the bass clef. This was a great shock to him.

The first piece my adult student Claire played to me on the piano was the Allegro, from Mozart's *Sonata in C major, K.545*. She was stuck with 'F A C E', another popular mnemonic for the notes on spaces in the treble clef. "I can't stop thinking of 'F A C E' " she admitted. She had to work out the letter name of every note in the bass clef by taking it up to the treble clef. After using 'F A C E' to name it, she would then count up two notes to name the bass clef note she wanted. Her original teacher just wanted to help her to 'enjoy music' and did her best to simplify music reading. However, this worked against Claire and as a result of the mnemonic method and over-use of *time savers* (see Chapter 11), she had given up playing piano for many years. After introducing her to the *key notes,* she now reads fluently and has now passed Grade 1 piano with distinction.

Ella was learning with another piano teacher and was due to take her Grade 4 exam in a few weeks - the week after her Grade 5 theory exam, for which I was teaching her in the latter stages. Fortunately, we were able to re arrange her piano exam for a Special Visit to give her some more preparation time, as she was unable to learn and play any of the scales or sight-reading at this level.

I found she was stuck with the 'cows' as I came to call it, in a similar way to Claire and she struggled to remember the fingering of the scales. Once I taught her to read music using the *key notes*, she was able to use the musical notation in the scale book to assist her with following the fingering provided. The scales became easier and so she liked them more. In just three weeks she was able to play all of the scales and in six weeks she went from a Grade 1 to Grade 4 level sight-reading. She was delighted to obtain a pass in both theory and Grade 4 piano.

If you are wondering how Ella knew her piano pieces and not her scales - apart from this being due to her excellent musical ear and being taught by 'rote' - read on.

Over-use of Time Savers

One sign for realising that the *key notes* can be useful is where teachers, in their efforts to help students learn pieces faster, have over-used *time savers* and so every note in the music has been named and fingered. One day a new student, Kaleb, arrived to have some extra piano lessons with me. He was not progressing with his current teacher who even said, "I think you need to start learning the notes."

I was very excited when I discovered that amongst the beginner pieces he had learned with his teacher, was a piece I had been looking for since I wrote about it in *Zoom88*. It was the song about a water tap, *Drip Drop,* which I told you about in the chapter 2. Kaleb was about to take his Grade 1 piano exam in a few weeks. I asked him to play *Drip Drop*. To my surprise he was unable to find any of the notes and could not play it at all. Concepts such as 'up' and 'down' were not understood. The reason was obvious. Each note on every piece of music had fingers numbers - *'time savers'* - written on them. Sadly, this young boy did not want to continue piano after he passed Grade 1.

I came to teach my adult student Zena when I found out that she was having difficulty accompanying her husband on the clarinet. She had passed her Grade 2 piano and yet she was unable to play a simple piece fluently. Even before I saw her music, I suspected the real problem could have been over-use of *time savers* and this proved to be the case.

I asked Zena to sight-read the left hand of a new piece. She paused and was wondering about the note G. "The grass....." she said. Fortunately, I knew exactly what was happening and what she meant. It was a case of 'All Cows Eat Grass' again. She had also been taught to work out the musical notes mainly by intervals. Months later she revealed that she was becoming more confident in all areas of her life through learning piano and cello with me, though she still felt that she was affected by her last teacher who got her to perform in music festivals. Although the adjudicators were very positive and kind, she had bad memories of her hands shaking uncontrollably as she was unable to read the music when she got stuck. Even though Zena can now read music, through using the *key notes*, she was still disturbed by these upsetting experiences until we did some TFT tapping. Now she can perform well and with confidence.

The father of one of my piano students told me he was stuck after Grade 4 on guitar. When he went on to Grade 5 theory he found he could only read music by association, with the guitar strings mnemonic 'Every African Dinosaurs Grow By Evolution.' Somehow he found a way to keep playing, unlike many others who get discouraged by the difficulties they encounter while reading music.

My sister Vivienne is a fluent music reader. Yet when I ask her how she knows that the note on the first line of the treble clef is an E, she says "Every Good Boy..."

So why do some people get stuck with the 'mnemonic cows' while others do not? I believe the reason for this is either the over-use of *time savers* or being taught only by 'rote.'

What causes getting stuck with the 'cows'?

As we often start to learn to read music when we are very young, many teachers do not know or understand why some students find it more difficult than others to learn musical notation or indeed exactly how they can help them.

The mnemonics are mistakenly thought to be an easier or quicker way to learn musical notes. In fact, they are slower and more confusing.

The seven 'deadly sins' of mnemonics for musical notation

Here are some issues that cause the use of mnemonics to make learning to read music more difficult for some people:

1. Always having to start at the beginning of the mnemonic.
2. There are too many variables causing confusion:
   - Lines or spaces?
   - Which clef is which?
   - Which mnemonic to use for which clef?
3. Too many different notes are used as 'anchors'.
4. There is no reference to pitch, direction, or how the notes relate to each other.
5. Mnemonics can lead to the habit of over-use of *time savers,* by writing in the letter names of each note.
6. They are abstract as they do not relate to music.
7. They cause dependency on the mnemonic.

Benefits of the Key Notes

What is the most fundamental and helpful note, missing in the mnemonics, that is in the *key notes*? Middle C.

What else do the *key notes* have that the mnemonics do not?
Both treble and bass clef staves are used simultaneously.

The *key notes* only use two letter names as an 'anchor'.

The *key notes* can help to identify any temporary or longer term problems students have with reversals of concepts in music, such as with letter names, clefs and direction of pitch. (See psychological reversal, Chapter 12.)

An adult student of mine, who was stuck with the 'cows' and 'F A C E' describes the benefits of using the *key notes*:

"Visually you can see middle C in the middle, connecting the treble and bass clef staves. There is less to remember with the key notes and you can work from there onwards."

Those of us who escaped getting stuck with the 'cows' or similar mnemonics are indeed fortunate. Still, for anyone reading this who is stuck or has a student who is having difficulty reading music, the message should be clear by now: help is at hand with the *key notes*.

My daughter Natalie, who I had taught piano up to Grade 3 standard, had then stopped playing this instrument. Twenty years later and now having a degree in psychology, she thought that apart from middle C, she would not remember how to read music and it could be too hard to do – one reason why she had not taken up the piano again.

Even though she claimed that she knew nothing about the 'cows' mnemonic, she asked about using the 'cows' notes.

Although she believed the *key notes* could be difficult to learn, with an open mind she started applying them and in minutes was reading Grade 1 standard pieces.

She suggested that the *key notes* could be written on tracing paper so they are nearer to the music to check, prior to knowing from memory.

The most important thing to remember or to bear in mind, is that learning to read music is a skill which takes time. It is a journey well worth pursuing.

Chapter 16
Top tips for Theory of Music

The cases of Ella and James in the previous chapter, *Cows, Clefs and Key Notes*, demonstrate just some of the reasons why it is best to take Grade 5 Music Theory well before it is needed for progress on to Grade 6 practical exam in ABRSM.

There are some students who complicate things and travel along 'side roads' rather than 'motorways' when applying music theory. Additionally, some need help with memory strategies, seeing patterns or following instructions. Plenty of practice is still needed, particularly with past exam papers.

The tips in this chapter can be applied to all levels of music theory. They can help improve performance whilst studying, as well as during the exam itself.

I guide students to work out their own corrections where possible, rather than write in the correct answer myself.

Be the Examiner – Check work done as if you are the examiner marking.

Be the inspector – Double check work done as if you are the inspector making sure the examiner has marked correctly.

B for Be Sure – the word 'GUESS' is crossed out.
Be as *sure* as you can be. Come back to answering a question later if necessary.

Clarity

Neatness counts. For example, it must be clear whether the note is an A or a G. Make it easy for the examiner to read.

Concentration and focus

Do theory work at a time and in a place where you can concentrate and focus well. Tap the PR spot (side of hand) if needed, even during an exam.

Musical knowledge, understanding and application

Some mistakes are made because there is more to learn through self-study or via your teacher.

Read the question carefully

Highlight key parts of the question; tick off these parts when you have answered them.

Reversals – getting things the 'wrong way round'.

For those students who have a tendency to encounter reversals - psychological reversal (see Chapter 12), in music theory there are many opportunities for such mistakes. Use TFT tapping reversal correction methods, such as the PR spot (side of hand). Another option is collarbone breathing.

Say Write:

Say the name of the note you want to write – aloud during study time, or silently inside your head during an exam. Now *write* it.

Slow – use appropriate ideas from Chapter 9 *Slow is Fast Progress.*

Steps Strategy – is about learning the order of the steps needed to complete the answers to questions. If something seems to be more difficult than usual or appears to be going wrong, go back to the first steps and review what you have done. Have you missed a step?

Support Tools
Make and use support tools for theory work, which you can reproduce on the additional paper provided in the exam. They can include things like the Key Notes, a hand drawn keyboard, methods for working out key signatures and chords.

Take Time - T.T.
Take Time to answer the questions. In the theory exam your knowledge of the theory of music is being tested, rather than how quickly you can complete the paper.

TFT tapping
Tap the *anxiety sequence* for exam nerves (see Appendix).

Write down all your working out.
This helps when you come to checking your work.

ZOOM!

Zoom in and take a close look at the music.
Zoom to the left, to the beginning of the bar or stave, in order to observe clefs, key signatures or accidentals.

Chapter 17
Name that tune

Are you a 'hummer' or know someone who is? Do you ever have 'earworms'- those catchy songs or tunes that go continuously round in your head?

I first became aware of my own earworms some years ago as I was leaving court number one at Wimbledon. Unaware that I was humming, a steward said to me, "Someone sounds happy!" My sister Vivienne then informed me that I had been doing this all the way through the last tennis game!

Later that year....

It was a frosty winter's night as we walked with our dog Candy.

"What are you singing?" my husband Laurence asked me, taking my humming to be a real song. This time he was right.

"We're all going on a *Summer Holiday*" I replied, adding the words to the tune made famous by Cliff Richard and The Shadows and amazing myself just what an earworm I had going round. It was certainly an unconventional way of keeping warm. I usually hum earworms when I am walking.

Another time, on a walk in our local park, Laurence asked me, "What song is that?" This time the earworm was a loop of something I had composed; a riff. In curiosity I took out a pencil and paper and wrote the short melody down.

Perhaps it is a form of what I call *musical doodles*; my unconscious composing, just like the unconscious drawing of my numerous doodles.

After all, composers are always looking for an original and memorable melody.

* * *

I am about to accompany Jane in a rehearsal at my home for her Grade 7 clarinet music exam. After so many years of working with musicians I finally meet my match. Jane enters the room humming!

In shock I greet her:

"It's so nice to meet another hummer. Do you often hum?" I ask her.

"All the time," she replies with her beaming smile.

The opening bars we play are not together. She has never played the piece with the piano before. I ask her to count aloud as I softly play the legato introduction; it is all out of time. I think there could be trouble ahead. I play it again really unmusically, accenting the beat for her to pick up. Success!

The music takes off and all is going well until later in the piece. Suddenly there are rhythmical problems again.

"I often have problems with rhythm," Jane announces.

She plays the bar again, with her foot tapping at a different time to the beat of the music.

"My teacher suggests I tap my foot to help me with the rhythm" Jane explains.

Now I realise the teacher has had problems teaching her.

I approach the music stand.

"How do you count this bar?" I ask

"De de deeee de deeee," Jane sings it.

I observe there are no numbers in the music; no *time savers* at all to remind her of certain places to count.

I quickly get her to explain that her clarinet teacher has demonstrated how this bar is to be played and Jane has simply copied her - by rote. Thus she never needed to learn how to count this bar. "It's much quicker and easier this way," Jane tells me.

Her music teacher has been unaware that this is how she is learning all her music. She has a very quick musical ear.

This is the reason why I usually demonstrate for my students only where it is essential and appropriate.

In seconds I show Jane how to count and write the numbers in the music. She quickly understands and the bar is now strictly in time.

Hearing her beautifully phrased, musical playing progress, I become more and more curious. I am not surprised when I ask about her musical background and she tells me she is working on Grade 8 piano and that she has relatives who are musicians, one a composer.

Hmm I think, composer, humming.

Chapter 18
"Why do advanced recorders have to play Carols?"

The early morning Rosh Pinah School advanced recorder group, in their enthusiasm, would sometimes arrive before me and begin playing their instruments. On one of these mornings as I walked upstairs to the music room, I could hear the familiar sounds of *Silent Night*. It was a duet from one of the recorder books, which they had chosen to play. As I entered the room, the last thing I wanted to do was stop the obvious pleasure they were having in their performance, so I allowed them to continue. The children told me how much they liked the music and were keen to play it again to me.

Of course, being a Jewish day school, playing a Christmas Carol was not the norm. We swiftly moved onto the next piece thinking nothing more about it.

The next day I was called into the Headmaster's office. It was the only disagreement I had with Mervyn Leviton. Sitting behind his desk in an obvious state of shock, anger and embarrassment, still recovering from a message on a small piece of blue paper with a parental complaint given to him by his secretary: "Mrs. Cohen wants to know why advanced recorders have to play Carols." Seemingly, on this occasion, he was siding with the parent in his complete astonishment about how this had happened.

I realised just what it was about this beautiful song and musical arrangement that the children had so enjoyed. So I set about composing a recorder duet for the group that was, in effect, a *re-composition*. Any residual anger on my part from my encounter with the Rosh Pinah Headmaster had been released and *Peaceful Days* (see Appendix) was born.

The children, completely unaware of how it had been composed, were delighted and keen to perform it in public. The next school event happened to be the festival of Shavuot[1], where the children dressed in white robes to re-enact the priests in the Temple. At one

---

[1] Shavuot marks the giving of the Torah to the Jewish people on Mount Sinai.

point in the ceremony, a recorder duet would traditionally be performed. *Peaceful Days* found its place and was heard annually thereafter at this celebration. As no one recognised its source, it became a closely guarded secret; that was until 2014 when I was working on this book and decided to include it and write about my experience of publishing my first composition. I wanted to find out if an eminent musician would recognise a famous song within it. Our friend Robert J. Sherman (son of Robert B. Sherman, composer of many famous Disney songs) was quick to spot a subtle clue in my duet.

I thought no more about my composition, until one day in July 2015 when I read a 'members news' notice in the ISM music journal *'Graham Lyons goes digital.' Graham Lyons, composer and inventor of the Clarineo, is interested in hearing from members who have written short and appealing pieces for budding instrumentalists, up to Grade 4 level.'*

I had known Graham from when I taught at the Jewish Free School (JFS); he was one of our peripatetic woodwind teachers. When we heard that he had invented the 'Lyons C clarinet', as it then was, my husband Laurence used this instrument with great effect for his students. However, we came to understand something had happened to Graham through the many difficulties of developing this instrument and we completely lost touch.

It was really strange and wonderful to be able to re-connect via his new website www.usefulmusic.com It was so exciting and such a surprise when I realised that, through Graham, I had now become a published composer - even before completing this book - with *Peaceful Days* arranged for flute and clarinet (as well as a flute duet)[2]. When I composed this piece I had no idea that I would play it on the flute and Laurence on the clarinet.

So at last those endless little earworms of mine made perfect sense - I was a composer in the making!

As a child I had sat at my Uncle Mick's piano and felt unable to make up any music or play by ear. He spurred me on to do this and I have subsequently encouraged my own students to do likewise.

---

[2] *Peaceful Days* duets for recorder, flute and for flute and clarinet are available as self-print PDFs from usefulmusic.com. Enter 'Peaceful Days' in the search bar.

My *Improvisation* and *Own Composition* (I.O.C.) triangle appears on many pages in their notebooks. Some students like to improvise during the warm-up at the beginning of their lessons.

- I = Improvisation: making music up and possibly forgetting what you have made up.
- O.C. = Own Composition: remembering the music you have made up. You can '*save*' it by recording it in some way.

Some ideas for composing music

Make a tune up for your telephone number.
Talking Fingers – a chit chat between right and left hands or high and low notes.
Theme and variations
Scale tunes
Black notes only – the pentatonic scale
The Musical Sandwich - ABA ternary form

RECOMPOSE (as *Peaceful Days)* – sometimes these can happen as 'musical accidents', see Chapter 12 *Mistaikes and Expectations.*

JOKES
Say then play - making up your own notes and rhythm. For example:
"What's a woolly sheep on a trampoline?"
"A woolly jumper."

COPY ME
Teacher copies student or vice versa
Left hand copies right hand or vice versa

BLENDING
Start a piece with a different one or before the end of a piece, start a new one.

WRITE MUSIC
Adam was a music student at the JFS, where I taught. He loved composing and writing 'symphonies'. At the time he was not able to hear or fully understand what he had written. However, he enjoyed it immensely and I am sure found it very therapeutic during a serious illness that he had. The British composer Mark-Anthony Turnage says he began composing in a similar way.

ABC
Choose at random three different letters of the musical alphabet and improvise music based on these notes. Any short melody, such as an original earworm, can be used in a similar way. From improvisation comes composition.

Chapter 19
The dotted rhythm

In this chapter, I will share with you how I teach the dotted crotchet-quaver rhythm:

When students clap this rhythm and count the beats aloud accurately, they will have more control and can play it correctly.

Example 1   Clap

Count   1   2 + 3

Example 2   Clap

Count   1   2 + 3

Example 3   Clap

Count   1   2 + 3

Step 1
Clap the rhythm and count the beats aloud, as in Example 1.

Step 2
Add a tie to the first crotchet, as in Example 2.
Clap the rhythm and count the beats aloud.

Step 3
Compare Example 2 with Example 3. The student should realise that the note lengths are the same, even though they look different. Clap the rhythm and count the beats aloud.

For beginners, I use the same approach to counting, even when the dotted crotchet-quaver rhythm appears on the second or third beat of the bar.

* * *

Master blaster

Carlos, an adult clarinet student, was having trouble co-ordinating his counting and clapping of the dotted crotchet-quaver and other rhythms. To help him, we effectively used collarbone breathing (see Appendix).

A few weeks later, he told me about his performance on the ancient musical instrument used in Jewish synagogue services – the shofar (ram's horn).

To play it well, as Carlos normally does, you need to fit the shofar precisely in your mouth and blow slowly and softly.

"On the first day of Rosh Hashanah (the Jewish New Year) the assistant Rabbi was watching and made me very nervous; he did not like my mistake at the start. This affected my playing, making it more complicated to blow.

During the silent part of the service, I put the shofar down and started the tapping exercises (collarbone breathing) and calmed myself down for the next round of blowing. I played much better, so I kept doing the tapping (PR spot, side of hand) before every time I had to perform."

Carlos described his experience as, "very interesting and insightful."

ZOOM 3

Selected cases

Chapter 20
Performance nerves in action

In December 1982 my career as a piano accompanist began in a dramatic way with Rachel, a Jewish Free School (JFS) pupil and one of my private piano students. She was also a competent trumpet player. It was the first time I was to accompany someone for an ABRSM exam. As I walked into the exam room for her Grade 3 trumpet exam, I was surprised to find the examiner was my former JFS music teacher, Mr Snary! Although we had kept in touch, I had not seen him since he had left the school some twelve years before.

To my horror, my previously confident student suddenly became extremely anxious - performance nerves in action. It was shocking and embarrassing; what would Mr Snary make of this?

I was impressed that Rachel did pass her exam, even though he commented on the mark form that 'some of the notes didn't speak or were inaudible'.

"My memory of all my music practical exams was extreme nervousness! It was worse for the trumpet (probably as my mouth would go dry) and it meant that every time I played in front of people I was only able to produce every other note! But I remember the examiner being very sympathetic and passing me despite the silences."[1]

My experience of feeling so helpless remained and inspired me to do more to handle such situations better in the future. Over the years I have told Rachel's story to candidates who have been upset after an exam, incorrectly thinking their musical slips would result in a failure.

---

[1] Email sent to author 30th May 2014

Chapter 21
Bertie to François

So far I have described strategies for preparing yourself or your students for a performance. My own story follows, the principle case history in this book. As you read it, you may well identify and learn from my own challenges and experiences.

INSPIRATION

Whilst accompanying various musical instrumentalists, including many on the flute, I found myself using the music and performance tips that I have covered in this book, together with the technical and breathing suggestions from my flautist friend, Chani Smith. In the autumn of 2006 while rehearsing with a Grade 6 flute candidate, I realised that as a 'beginner' on this instrument, I could make a better sound than she did when I gave her a demonstration. I was asked a number of times by various parents of these candidates whether I taught the flute. This question, combined with my growing love of accompanying a piece called *Bertie's Blues* by Paul Hart, made me decide to come back to playing this instrument. I purchased a better flute and was now ready to progress and fulfil my childhood dream. Passionate about sharing this with you, I decided to keep a journal in the run up to my Grade 8 flute.

PREPARATION JOURNAL FOR GRADE 8

GRADES 3-7, A RESUME

I am overwhelmed by the scale book and quickly get stuck. I do not know what the small circles are above some of the notes. I am a student without a teacher, being typically impatient to play and do not read the printed instructions carefully enough. While others are watching Christmas TV, I find an alternative; using my musical experience and teaching techniques, in a very disciplined way, I set out on the journey of mastering the flute.

In February 2008, some weeks before my Grade 3 flute exam, I am on the slopes of Slovenia with my ski instructor, waiting in the long half - term queue for the ski lift. I think we could have a conversation about peak performance as he used to ski in his National Team. Our conversation is short - lived. He has just one word to say: '*Preparation*'.

Now it is just one week to go before my exam. I find it hard to pick up the phone to arrange and make time for a lesson with flute teacher Carolyn Davidov, whose students I have often accompanied. It is also one of the most important decisions I make. Specialist instrumental advice is necessary and it is always useful to be the student of a teacher again. As a music teacher, I am aware that there are high expectations and some self-imposed pressure to do well.

During an exam so much concentration is needed for our own performance. A distraction becomes a mini exam trauma during my Grade 5 flute exam in spring 2009, when I am asked the wrong scale by the examiner. I discover music examiners are human and can make mistakes.

In 2012, the Olympics are held in London. At the beginning of the year I begin the *Weekly Rhythm Record* (see Appendix) to track and record music practice. I am going for my own 'musical Olympics', Grade 6 flute. In my exam, a few months later, I feel rushed into commencing playing; my warm up is interrupted with: "Now let's hear the Allegro". When I announce my piece as 'Largo and Allegro' the examiner does a quick rearrangement of her papers, "Oh yes, you are not doing Grade 5, you are doing Grade 6'. Then during my scales the examiner asks *me*: "Now which is it, *slurred* or *tongued*? Oh yes, we did *tongued* before, so *slurred* please".

By 2013 I am progressing with the flute when one day I suddenly decide to play my cello and do not want to stop. A few days later I am just at the end of a Pilates class when I realise, too late, that I have been ignoring the mild pain I have been experiencing over the week in my right shoulder. I have tendonitis in my right shoulder. It is a cruel reminder of my suffering from RSI as a music student. It is so bad that I think I will not be able to play the flute again. However, with Self-Hypnosis, Thought Field Therapy (TFT), Physio and resting, I recover and learn to use my own advice and techniques to protect myself from this happening again.

Seeing how tense I get and how much I have to put in to achieve Grade 5, my husband Laurence thinks it is enough that I have got to this stage. He certainly expects me to stop at Grade 6. So I decide to go through Grade 7 myself with my teacher Carolyn and not do the actual exam. I wonder if I also want to avoid having more of those mini exam traumas? For my Grade 8 I am determined that it will be a more gradual journey and that tension from previous grades will be left behind.

In April 2015 I write my top personal goals, *Zoom88* (this book) and my Grade 8 flute. At the end of September once again I get over that step of making the call to arrange lessons with Carolyn. I am told about the difficulty of the many scales. I am determined to put in all the work that I need to in order to master these, including more performance practice. Carolyn asks me to play a scale *tongued*. In the syllabus it is called *legato-tongued*. I am wondering how many other woodwind and brass teachers are aware of this. Apparently I have also chosen one of the more technically challenging Mozart flute concerto movements, the third movement of the *Flute Concerto no.2 in D major, K.314 Allegretto malincolico* - the first movement of the Poulenc *Sonata*, is very exciting; it feels like a story in the making. Francis (not François) Poulenc was composing his Sonata for flute and piano in 1956, the year I was born. I can hardly believe I am playing the piece I have enjoyed accompanying for years. It is like a dream coming true.

By November it is time to decide whether I will take the exam at the end of this term or in March. I want to take it in December and am shocked to hear myself say, "I want to get it over with" simply so I can focus on writing this book.

6ᵗʰ November D-42 (42 Days to exam day)

'D Day' - Decision Day – arrives, although it is fourteen days before the actual date when I need to enter. I am about to go to my lesson after a good long warm - up. I seem to be blowing raspberries rather than notes on those octave leaps and harmonics. Is it nerves or lack of technique? I am grateful for remembering *to tap the PR spot*, what a *Time Saver* - the raspberries disappear.

As I am asking Carolyn for some advice as to when I should take my exam, I can hear the voices of various music students' parents, as well as some of my adult students, wanting me to enter them or their child for exams before they are really ready. My pass rate for entering my own students or accompanying others has been 100% for many years. Carolyn tells me that it is my decision and it depends on how much pressure I want. To me it is more about motivation. Right now my motivation level is very high. However, I can hear my piano teacher Eva saying, "What is the hurry?"

Carolyn, who got to know Sir James Galway when they were at Music College together, is doing what she can to help me get the best tone with the widest range of dynamics. She is often telling me how 'Jimmy' would do it. I put as many of these tips as I can into practice. I am enjoying the process.

Flute is 'me time'; it takes me, like writing, into another world. It is a wonderful place.

I employ Laurence as my *musical slow coach* to help me with the scales. "Your fingers, tongue and brain are all going in different directions when you are playing too fast" he observes. I introduce him to my *slow lesson*. I tell Laurence that I need to *Take Time* before starting my scales. I show him my *musical secretary lesson* when he hears me 'spitting' instead of producing one of the notes. When I get it right he says, "Green for GO, you are ready to go on now."

I realise Carolyn is asking me to play at the exam tempo and standard, with correct breathing included, while I am still mastering the fingering and embouchure and position of moving the flute as I play. Many different skills are being mastered.

I begin to understand why I am going too fast. It is *expectations*.

I use my *learning; the A--B line* and on the scales I begin again at *A* - back at nursery, going slowly, practising and using my *successipe*.

Laurence and I are in Eva's kitchen, doing a *musical slow coach lesson* after chatting with her about the importance of slow practice. Many of my learnings about this come from her. "It is why many people do not play well. They get bored and do not have the patience to practise slowly." Eva says. Somehow I have the patience; I just need encouragement and my *musical slow coach*. Really that is Laurence and myself.

D-35

Carolyn says she would love it if all her students would improve like I have and with the same level of commitment. *I trust this book will help you or your students to achieve this.* First I am working on using the ideas and techniques for myself. Of course I know that they will work, as in a variety of different ways they have all come from my own experience in the first place.

I really enjoy putting my pieces together for the first time with my piano accompanist, Elizabeth Tyler, five weeks before exam day. She recognizes I am 'bold and brave' in arranging this. I am impressed that if there are any slips, she notices the real mistake on the last page of the Poulenc: two notes in one bar that I misread. I know immediately how this has happened. I had not used *Say Play* and the *Zoom lesson* here; Carolyn has not yet heard this somewhat easier part of the piece and even the small amount of work I have done on it means I have been practising mistakes.

Carolyn would rather I take the exam next term, yet somehow I am unable to get 18th December out of my head. We agree that I mainly need to increase the speed over the next few weeks and keep improving musically. I decide to use as many of the *A-Z handbook of music lessons* (Chapter 8) and the *A-Z handbook on learning and practising* (Chapter 11) as I can. I am trusting that my own *Zoom88* book can help. Now it is not only Molly-Ann Smith who suggests ABRSM could publish my book, it is Carolyn as well.

It is time to let Carolyn hear how I am getting on with the sight-reading. She picks out the most challenging test she can find. At aged fifty-nine I am surprised to find myself learning to read music again; I am still working on reading those top notes where there are so many ledger lines. When I scan the Sight-Reading test, I am more concerned about those notes than anything and think the rhythm simple. How wrong I turn out to be; Carolyn stops me half way and points out my rhythmical error. I realise I need to use my *Sight-Reading chart* (see Appendix) and stick to its order of priorities next time. Once again it is a case of using my own lessons for myself.

D-32

For a few days I work on eliminating a Repetitive Strain Injury (RSI), again in my right shoulder. Sitting badly at the computer for too long is the last straw after a day of my maximum practice so far of ninety minutes. I am now basing my exam entry decision on how well I recover. I use the TFT *pain sequence*, some *massage* from my daughter Natalie, a few *physio exercises*, along with some *Heat Lotion* and *MSM gel*, as well as *resting*. I am delighted with my speedy recovery and yet again learn to be careful of the other things I do around playing a musical instrument.

Suddenly my low D and C notes are not working. For several minutes I struggle to produce their sound. What is wrong with my flute? I am taken back to when my student's flute broke when I was accompanying him during his Grade 8 exam. I *tap a TFT sequence for this past trauma*. The notes mysteriously work again.

D-28

It is exam entry day. I am so excited. I actually feel like I have passed my exam today, not just entered it. It is such an achievement even to get to this point. I partly get Carolyn's blessing: "You will be even better if you leave it to next term." I appreciate her high standards. I tell her I have got four weeks to go until my exam. The truth is, I am now so focused and am unstoppable. I tell Laurence the news: "This is the last one; do not tell me you are checking the syllabus for harmonica exams, or that you are now going to do Grade 2 on the recorder."

Eva reminds me to take the opportunity to play to as many people as I can. I do this, even if it is just playing a scale to my music students. It is good for them to know how I have to practise. Eva also advises me: *"Do not practise on the day of the exam; it is already too late. The practice must be done before. Just play the pieces once, slowly."*

D-25

It is a freezing cold day and I burn my lips on a hot drink. I am grateful for my Lip Balm, which speedily heals them.

D-20

I fall up the stairs in my excitement to get back to watch the Murray brothers make history as they play doubles together for Great Britain in the Davis Cup. A short *TFT sequence for pain* on my wrist and a *hot and cold rinse under the tap* and I am back practising my flute again. I remind myself to use the *slow lesson* in life at the moment.

One thing is for sure: through my Grade 8 flute I have greatly increased my appreciation of great flute playing by the masters. I was fortunate enough to hear James Galway play in a concert with the RPO at the Royal Festival Hall, 10th June 1979, in which he played four encores, two of them for solo flute.

Now I am watching him on YouTube and seeing and hearing so much more. There is really nothing quite like learning the actual instrument oneself to get a deeper understanding and appreciation. I am now also appreciating, more than ever, the expertise and sounds of live music making, even on different instruments.

D-18

It is a bit like parting with my baby to let my flute have a small repair done. Still, I know how important it is to ensure my instrument is in tiptop condition.

I get the A and G pads fixed. It does make a difference and it is easy to get the highest and lowest notes now.

Laurence gives me a *Jigsaw lesson* in the kitchen; while he is eating his fruit salad, I practise my scales and realise I simply need to conserve my breath to get that top note at the end of the Scale of C major.

With just over two weeks to go to my exam, the important thing is that I am feeling calm and enjoying the process of my flute journey and how it is all coming together. It is a wonderful feeling when the music begins to feel 'easy' to play.

D-16

At my rehearsal with my accompanist, Elizabeth, she tells me the demonstration of TFT tapping I gave her last session - PR spot (side of hand) and collarbone breathing (see Appendix) has helped her to recover from an irritating cough, which had left her sleep-deprived.

As for my playing today, "It just needs to be polished now" she says and I agree with her. When more absorbed in the music, she notices I play with more dynamic range. There is a great sense of achievement to be able to play and perform Poulenc all the way from *Berties Blues*. It is amazing how I have got here.

So, what am I putting aside you may wonder? Whatever it is, it is not this book. It has been continuing throughout my Grade 8 preparations. Yes, it is all about preparation. I am determined to know all the scales as well as I can and avoid any of the all too common 'scale traumas'; like the one where my son David nearly did not attend his Grade 8 trumpet, for which he got a distinction, as not all the scales were known.

As for the aural, I am enjoying the challenge. I am wondering as I write this, when did you last do an aural test yourself? For some of the tests I hear myself saying, "This is easy" and then realise I have relaxed too much as I have not checked the question or concentrated enough. For describing the characteristic features of a piece of music played by the examiner, test D: in my head I think of some answers and they are good. I need to remember to say those things and trust my musical instincts, just as I tell my students.

I am grateful for being able to use my perfect pitch in the aural. I had been unaware that I had this ability when I first used it to my advantage when at my senior school, JFS; I had matched the sound of the 'pips', the sound that meant it was the end of a lesson, on the descant recorder. On more than one occasion, unknown to our musical form teacher Mr Snary, I blew the 'pips' in order for our class to be let out of school early. It was only at aged sixteen, when learning cello with Raphael Wallfisch, that I found out I had perfect pitch. I am putting it to good use now.

D-14

Carolyn is impressed with how I have kept my record of practice in the *Weekly Rhythm Record*. I think she is telling me I am on track for my Grade 8 and that my playing must be improving, as she is talking to me about what I would need to do for the Diploma. I tell her that this book must be written first. Meanwhile I am putting *Zoom88* into practice. Every lesson I come with a few questions, the *Ask your teacher lesson*. It is time well spent.

Carolyn "loves" the cadenza I compose for the second largo in the Telemann *Fantasia in B minor* and wants me to make her a copy. How on earth will I write it so that someone will be able to play the rhythm as I do? At least there will be a record of what I play. I am very happy to hear she likes it so much. Maybe I can take those earworms and my composition more seriously in the future.

Laurence offers to listen to my scales, an offer I want to make the most of, as there was no time in my lesson with Carolyn today. They are not as good as before. He suggests me playing the pieces through to him for the first time. I have played them better. I remember *to tap my PR spot and things change*. This is good practice for what to do in my exam should I need it; to remember that if such a thing happens, I need to do something to turn it round quickly. There is always something one can do.

D-11
The hardest aspect of my Grade 8 flute, apart from getting a reasonable sound on the tops notes, as opposed to a screech, is mastering the ledger lines. I compose little fragments of melodies on the ledger lines so as to get used to reading these notes. Have I spotted a gap in the market? Even with my *Key Notes* and *composing*, it is still work in progress with less than two weeks to go.

I am making too many mistakes when I am doing my practice performances. A *Mistakes Lesson* is needed, along with most of *Theme and Variations* - my *A-Z handbook of music lessons*. I just have no need for my *overcoming procrastination to practise lesson* as I am so motivated - the value of doing an exam; it helps one to go to the highest level of performance possible at the time. Now I am regularly practising several times a day; it is the easiest thing to do. Like with the writing of this book, time is my friend. I know the more time I put in, the more sure I am that I will get there.

D-10
I read chapter 12 *Mistaikes and expectiations* and find it useful. I have been beating myself up and welcome a reminder that the frustrations of those mistakes are really about learning what needs to be done. They are a necessary part of practising, so one knows how to improve the performance.

D-8
I place my S.U.M.*O. boxing glove* in sight of my music stand.

I am so much calmer today. "Where did all those mistakes fly away to?"

I begin to realise that I can easily get confused with the instructions and terminology used for playing the scales. There is, after-all, so much to think about anyway, apart from which notes to play. The idea is that by now everything should be automatic. Still, with Laurence acting as my mock examiner, I am finding that being asked which scale I should play and how I should play it, can sometimes be a bit much to process.

Suddenly there is déjà vu from chapter 1 of this book, as I notice I am asking myself: *"Legato or Slurred?"* Will the examiner ask me to play *legato* or *slurred*? I am translating that for *slurred* scales I should play *legato* and for *legato-tongued* scales I should play *smooth* and *tongued*. Fortunately I think the *staccato* is straightforward. When Laurence sometimes asks me to play a scale *'tongued'* I correct him and ask him to always say *'legato-tongued.'* Confusing as it is, I know I need to get used to the exact terminology printed in the syllabus.

I am very fortunate that Laurence works from home and has his own personal interests. Whilst his encouragement is vital, at a time like this I am particularly grateful to him for giving me plenty of quiet time and space to practise.

D-7

We begin my flute lesson today with a special kind of warm-up and through it achieve one of my goals - playing a flute duet for the first time with Carolyn. This goal helped motivate me to get to Grade 5, as she had told me there were some lovely flute duets at this level. Somehow I have bypassed playing these. Instead, today we play my composition, *Peaceful Days* (see Appendix). Carolyn says, *"It is beautiful, lovely long phrases and I love the title. You should get it published and write more."*

We use the *Affirmation lesson*: together we work out the words for an affirmation to assist with my scales: "I can get those top notes when I tighten my diaphragm."

Carolyn is impressed with the first page of the Poulenc where I have spent much time practising, in the lessons and at home. She has also noticed how little time I have spent on the last page of this piece. However, she did not know that I had spent a very long time on three particular notes on this page, as by now they are so fluent. There are a few of my A-Z *handbook of music lessons* that I am aware of Carolyn giving me. For example, the *Fussy Lesson* appears often.

D-4

I play the Poulenc to Eva. It is not up to scratch. She asks me if I really need to take the exam on Friday. My answer is a definitive "yes". After having a wonderful *slow lesson* on this piece from Eva - my original *musical slow coach*, the Mozart and Telemann go much better and she can only make the smallest of suggestions. Tonight I work hard on the Poulenc.

D-3

My last lesson before the exam and Carolyn is going on again about the diploma. Meanwhile, Laurence is expressing relief that "this is the last exam".

D-2

A wonderful feeling envelops me as I am rehearsing for the third time with my accompanist. My plan is to really 'get into the music' today and let go of all the technical stuff. It works; as I play the Poulenc I can hear myself saying "I *love* this music – *show* it". All I want is to have this wonderful feeling when performing to others.

In the last few days before the exam I manage to get the practising up to two hours a day. I am appreciating good health, though I notice that sometimes when I play the flute, under my right jaw there is something going on; there is an occasional ache. Whatever it is, it seems unconnected to my practising and I decide it has to wait until after my exam to be sorted out.

D-1

I am somewhat in a state of disbelief that I have actually got this far. I am calm and excited, looking forward to tomorrow, when there is a slight panic; suddenly a note does not work properly. Again, it feels like it was yesterday when that student's flute broke during his exam. My SUD (Subjective Units of Distress) is ten. I quickly go down to a zero after tapping a *TFT sequence* for another layer of that *past trauma*. I find myself saying "So what, focus on *now*!" Again, misterioso, the note works.

Although I am somewhat puzzled and frustrated by the slips in my performance, I know it is related to my preparation rather than being performance anxiety. I am happy with my 'pass' level of preparation and more than pleased to get to this point in such a healthy state, having achieved so much in this way.

Today I am performing at Hill House Care Home to a resident who is a good friend of my mother. When I look round, care staff have gathered behind me to listen; it leads me to imagine I am playing in some huge park to the world. Afterwards my mother gestures with a horizontal line moving upwards to show me just how much progress she has heard me make.

My dream to play the flute, from when I was eleven years old, is about to reach a very important milestone.

Chapter 22
Tongued or staccato?

The tale of the entranced examiner

BEFORE

It is the morning of my Grade 8 flute exam, 18th December 2015. *I focus on the task in hand* – final preparations for what feels more like my launch into Space than my exam.

All seems to be calm as I go about my warm-ups. Then I find something strange on the carpet; it is round, flat and a whitey green in colour. At this moment it only looks like one of my flute pads, as if confirming any fears of having problems with the condition of my instrument. In reality it is probably just a squashed pea!

Clearly, still being affected by a past musical trauma and knowing we can attract what we fear or focus on, action is needed. Like a butterfly, flying in with a sudden thought, *one of these kinds of Thought Fields needs tapping away.* So I do a TFT sequence for my fear of the flute breaking during the exam, as had happened when I was accompanying a student for *his* Grade 8 flute exam. The fear vanishes.

Apart from playing my flute, I do anything – walk in the park, read, relax, trim my fringe - other than using a computer. I want to ensure I have maximum energy and concentration.

Slow practice is easy today. *Slow* is my friend. Eva Bernathova, my piano teacher, has drilled me: "*Only slow practice on the day. Do everything slowly.*" I am doing so. For this grade, I will take my time on the warm-up in the exam room. I am using a Neuro-Linguistic Programming (NLP) technique called *Future Pacing,* a type of mental rehearsal.

Laurence can hear the sounds of those scales coming from our music room. There is a knock on the door. "*Make sure you don't do too much*" he gently reminds me. However, my split-up hour of practice is nearly done. It is a nice, yet quite strange feeling to know that the intense scale practice is at an end.

"How is it that I am so calm? How do I do it?" I am not a notorious nervous adult taking a music exam. *What tips and tools can I pass on to help those who are nervous?*

Briefly I look forward to my post-exam goals, the rewards. Then, considering my most useful warm-ups, I recall a conversation: "How are you so relaxed today?" I had once asked one of my candidates who I was accompanying on their exam day. They replied: "I lay down on the floor before I came here and did some breathing." It was the *diaphragmatic breathing* I had shown them how to do in rehearsal.

Right now I have a slight pain on the right side just under my ribs. I decide to lie on the floor myself, do some of this breathing and a *Progressive Muscle Relaxation*. The pain disappears.

I make sure I have only eaten a small amount. I apply some *Aloe* to ensure my lips are completely smooth, have a sip of water and set off to the exam. I am wondering: "What difference is there between nerves and excitement?" Where does one start and the other begin? I do not feel nervous, so am I just a little bit excited? My heart is beating faster as I park outside the exam centre, the home of my flute teacher Carolyn Davidov.

'*I always say a prayer before a performance.*' says Sir James Galway. It feels like I am doing the same. I am two minutes early, so there is enough time to do my planned *palming*[1] in the car. My heartbeat returns to normal.

I am now reading a sign on Carolyn's front door from the examiner: '*Best wishes for an enjoyable and successful exam.*' I like the word *successful* and decide to take it inside with me. I already have the *enjoyable* word with me.

I have planned to include the Marcel Moyse *De La Sonorite - Art Et Technique* and just a few more of those lovely scales in the warm-up room. However, my accompanist Elizabeth Tyler joins me and I quickly adapt my plan when she says "I am just worried about the tempo." Worried? She is always so relaxed. I want my accompanist to be as calm as I am. I suggest doing some tapping together. She happily agrees to do this with me only after I had reassured her that there would indeed be time. We tap a short TFT sequence for anxiety, followed by the *PR spot* (side of hand) and just the major

---

[1] The Bates Method - Palming Technique

part of the sequence for *visualising peak performance* (see Appendix).

DURING

Carolyn gives me a final reminder: "full warm, rich tone" as I enter the exam room with Elizabeth. I am comfortable wearing my musical T-shirt, the outfit in which I have given my best practice performance. The examiner has a broad friendly smile. She immediately puts me at my ease as she gives me the choice as to whether I include two short cadenzas in the Mozart flute concerto. She seems pleased when I tell her I have made a cut in the piano accompaniment from twenty two to ten bars. I hand her a small card with the details of my programme, something I know examiners appreciate. *Icebreakers* and *Time Savers* are over.

After tuning with the piano, I do a brief warm-up, the first few notes of the seasonal Carol, *Noel*. I wonder if she notices, or is she too busy preparing her papers? I want to check some other top notes, so I go un-seasonal and play the beginning of *Hot Cross Buns*, ensuring a beautiful top C. All those notes are sounding good and there is no spitting like I heard briefly in the warm-up room.

My first piece, *Allegretto malincolico* - the first movement of the Poulenc *Sonata* - starts quite well. I curse myself momentarily that I did not play the top F sharp on page two. I wonder how convincing my alternative note was? Should I have stuck with Carolyn's suggestion of fingering which was still only 80% reliable? Or would my idea of a different fingering have been fine had I discovered it some days earlier? This is no time for such an internal conversation and I am very quickly 'back in the music'.

I end the piece well in control of what I want to achieve musically. I have a sip of water and retune, *taking time* to get ready for the next piece.

Although my intention is to get a pass, as I am performing my second piece, the 3rd movement of the Mozart *Flute Concerto no.2 in D major, K.314*, I am telling myself that this 'merit-standard' playing. I feel I am in a very peaceful and special place; somewhere that no one else could enter. It is a place where, in this state of relaxed concentration, I can play my best.

I am tempted to continue on to the third piece; then I remember the plan I have made with Carolyn for me to do the aural next. "Stick with it" I can hear myself saying. We had arranged this for good reasons.

Singing the lowest part of a three-part phrase for Test A, my left ear could have been more prepared to focus on that bass line and filter out all other sounds as I can do. The identification of cadential chords comes next. It is known to be the most challenging element of the aural. I hesitate: is there a seventh in that dominant chord? I think not. The examiner appears to be aware of my reason for taking that extra moment to identify this chord.

The sight singing, Test B, is usually easy for me. However, today there is an interval that sounds rather strange when the examiner accompanies me. I am singing it again after the test as she gives me an understanding smile. There is no time for uncertainty in the aural; one just has to keep moving on. Having perfect pitch, the modulations in Test C are straightforward. At least I am certain of something.

I am happy that the period of composition for the piece in Test D is clear. Yet because it is familiar, it has stunned me; I remind myself that I still need to talk about its characteristic features. I invite the examiner to stop me when she has heard enough of my description, which she does.

A few music bars into playing the Telemann *Fantasia in B minor*, I am shocked to hear the sound of a mobile phone going off. It is on 'silent and vibrate' and seems amplified. "Is it coming from the kitchen? Has it been left in a bag in the exam room itself, somewhere near the door?" I go around the room in my mind, attempting to locate the source of the sound. Then I realise to my horror it could actually be my *own* mobile phone; coming right through the ceiling from my music bag in the waiting room above. How is this possible? I glance at the examiner who does not flinch or look at all perplexed by the uninvited sounds. She appears transfixed as she watches me. I go on performing, acting as if nothing has happened.

I think of Eva, who continued playing the piano in a concert during an earthquake. She was thought of as a heroine at the time. Now it is my turn to be a heroine. After all, it is 'just' a mobile phone. These thoughts help me to put things in perspective and keep concentrating as much as I can.

The Toccata-like *Vivace* is normally followed immediately by an *Allegro*, a Gigue. However, I am too shocked and curious to realise that I should go straight on. I need to ask the examiner a question: "Did you hear the mobile phone ringing?" She did not and clearly thought I might have had concerns, as she immediately reassures me that it has not affected my performance at all.

After this extended pause I am about to move swiftly onto the Gigue. However, the examiner is moving on to the next part of the exam. Somewhat confused I ask her, "Would you like to hear the Gigue?" She apologises, explaining that there is so much repertoire for them to know and kindly invites me to play it. Fortunately all goes well and I am glad I have included it, after all the practice I have done.

My aim is to *take time* and only start to *play each scale after three to five seconds.* I had felt rushed in previous flute exams; the pace is always fast, being asked the different scales in succession, one after another. I would be happy for the examiner to give me a comment like 'a rather slow or cautious response today'.

Although Carolyn had suggested that if I made more than one mistake I could ask to play the scale again, the examiner gives me no chance; straight away the next scale is requested. "I could play those high notes better" I think. C'est la vie; perhaps during the pieces I have shown this.

The articulation requirements for Grade 8 flute scales are *slurred, legato-tongued* or *staccato.* When the examiner asks me to play a scale *tongued,* as I am playing I realise I am doing *staccato.* So now I find myself in a state of confusion: '*tongued* or *staccato?*' Needless to say the scale was hesitant due to my uncertainty. I clarify with the examiner that she has meant *legato-tongued.* To my relief I notice afterwards that she used the correct terminology and I am back on my automatic response.

However, there was yet another confusion that I became aware of during the scales that I had never noticed before: The examiner says, "and now I am going to ask you some scales". That means first major, then minor *scales* and later major, then minor *arpeggios.* In lessons and practice at home, this had meant all the different types of scales. The effect is that the examiner has fewer words to say and the candidate less time to think what they are going to play. It makes it even speedier than has been practised. Instead of 'C major *scale*' or

'C major *arpeggio*', the candidate just hears 'C major'. That one missing word can make a big difference.

Suddenly as I begin to play C# minor *arpeggio* I am thinking: "she did ask me to play an arpeggio and not a scale didn't she?" Now I am confusing '*scale or arpeggio?*' I stop and clarify this with the examiner before continuing.

It is at this moment that I realise our preparations had been too harsh. We had been jumping from scales to *arpeggios* and other types of scales rather than just doing it in the order as in the syllabus. The examiner asking the scales in order should make it easier, yet because we have not prepared ourselves (or our students) in such a way, it makes it harder in the exam as we are waiting for a further instruction that is not coming.

I am quite surprised that throughout my exam, any concerns I had experienced about breath control issues or getting clogged up with saliva during practice have simply not occurred. *I am in a deep state of relaxation and my breathing is most comfortable.* It is indeed a good feeling. I had rehearsed how to cover up my mistakes and today I have covered them up much better than I did in practice performances. In general I am feeling that I have played the best I can at this point in time. What more can one want?

I waste the first few seconds of viewing of the Sight-Reading test. I suddenly realise I am simply staring at the first notes as if waiting for an instruction or signal as what to do next. Now I know I have limited time to work out those high notes on the ledger lines. I suffer from this happening and, during the performance, fluff several of them. I could have done with some tapping before this test to help with reading those ledger line notes more speedily. Then there is an unusual rhythmic pattern with a rest and a triplet that throws me. The exam has ended, yet I find myself staring at the Sight-Reading, still working that rhythm out.

The time has flown by and I cannot believe thirty minutes have passed so quickly.

AFTER

I go straight to my music bag in the waiting room and find my mobile phone. There is a missed call at 12.10pm. I suggest to Carolyn that in future she should advise people to turn *off* their phones in the waiting room. I sit for a few minutes while putting my flute away, as I recover from the excitement. A conversation I overhear reminds me of two words I had written down for tips *on the day: 'be yourself'*.

I tell Carolyn "I am moving on, whatever the result" and tell Elizabeth: "I am not doing it again in March". I feel confident that I have passed. I would be really happy if it could end with simply being told this right now. I do not need anything else. I have achieved everything I wanted and do not want to spoil this lovely feeling.

Back home, my daughter Natalie says "Now you get to massage me without having to practise your flute." She no doubt remembered how many massages got delayed when I 'just have to practise my flute first'. It is a reminder of the inevitable sacrifices, things one needs to put aside in order to achieve one's goals.

The best thing has been my preparation. It worked so well and this is why I am so happy. The worst thing was that I had no time to read over my *on-the-day* notes in the warm - up room and I forgot to tap in between the scales. This was frustrating, as I know it would have helped me to perform better and get a few more marks. I forget to tap for frustration, as I am so happy about everything else. It has been a really good experience just to focus on something like this. It reminds one what can be achieved by doing so.

I feel quite elated – like on another planet! So maybe I did take off into 'space' after all. I realise that the whole exam was conducted free of any physical pain. That is an achievement in itself. As the celebrations begin, I become aware that not only had my flute been in perfect condition, I had completely forgotten my fear of it breaking during the exam.

Over a week later I am having a few days rest from the flute, as I become increasingly aware of an ache under my right jaw. I suddenly wonder if I had strained it in those final days before my exam. Finally after quizzing myself over and over again as to whether I needed to see my doctor - for a lump, or my dentist - for a tooth problem, I decide to tap a TFT sequence for pain when I catch that ache bothering me. It disappeared immediately and I was both relieved and bemused.

I am surprised when I realise I have had just ten flute lessons for this grade as well as the three rehearsals with my accompanist. I am expecting the certificate I feel I deserve; perhaps to open yet more doors for me to help others enjoy my flute music. I *visualise* writing, and sharing the picture of my certificate: 'look what came in the post today'. As this date gets nearer, the thought comes into my mind more frequently. It feels like a race to complete writing this chapter before that email or the large white envelope with a certificate and mark form arrives.

2nd January 2016. I begin to get that nervous excitement whenever I open my emails. However, for that moment when one actually gets the confirmation, yes, it is that feeling again: "What difference is there between nerves and excitement?" They are once again very closely linked and mixed together.

7th January, the email finally arrives. Laurence and I open it together with great excitement. It is a distinction, 130 marks. "Oh my goodness! It (the A-Z in my book) works!" I am shocked and delighted at the same time. I had never achieved a distinction at this level in either my piano or cello exams. Now my excitement turns to those this book could help through me sharing my ideas and experiences.

9th January, look what *has* arrived in the post. My certificate and mark form. It reads *'prompt response'* for the scales. Aural: *'The responses were confident'*. I must surely have done what I teach others – *act confident*, even if you do not feel it. To my surprise the only aural test I got wrong is one of the two modulations.

"Very impressed with the report form. Very well done. I was thrilled with your result so much so that I opened a bottle of champagne last night that I had been saving. It is not every day a distinction at Grade 8 is achieved. Wish you had been here to share a glass. We must get together for the duets. All the best. Carolyn"[2]

The next door is opening.

---

[2] email sent to author 11.1.16

Chapter 23
Is there a bee in the classroom?

In helping students do their best in music lessons, I have found myself using complementary methods to treat anything from hiccups to headaches; as one of them wrote:

"The more I tapped for my headache, the more it improved. It was a miracle!"

There can be unusual reasons for lack of progress or difficulties in performing.

A teenage boy, Yoni, was preparing for his Grade 7 cello exam. One of the pieces was called *The Clown*. He was not progressing well with it. There seemed to be no obvious reason, until I discovered that he had a phobia of clowns, which had begun when he was a young child. After treating this, his performance of the piece was immediately transformed. Unfortunately, he also suffered badly from hay fever, which affected his intonation.

This case, as with so many others, shows that there are reasons for progress being blocked. A twelve-year-old girl, Tracey, came to me for cello lessons having already learned the instrument for two years. I was told she was suffering from emotional problems caused by bullying, as well as some medical issues.

I quickly established she had problems with intonation and needed some help understanding rhythm. During one lesson, Tracey was unable to play a simple note of a piece she knew quite well. She told me that she was distracted as she was singing in a concert that evening and was feeling nervous. After tapping a TFT sequence for her anxiety about wanting to be 'perfect', her level of concern dropped rapidly and she was able to continue playing her cello normally. From this day on, if Tracey arrived at her lesson feeling physically uncomfortable – with stomach pain, nausea or headaches – or emotionally upset in some way, we would first treat these symptoms so she was more comfortable and could concentrate on her playing. For example, one day Tracey was unable to perform her sight-reading as well as usual. She told me she was having intrusive thoughts about the safety of a friend. After tapping a TFT sequence for this, she remarked, "it helps clear my mind."

She spent a limited amount of time practising. On discussing this it became evident that there were environmental reasons for this.

Despite this, we pressed on and started preparing Tracey for Grade 1. Week by week there would be some progress; it was a slow and very gradual process. Most weeks I would gently encourage Tracey to stretch the fingers of her left hand to get the notes in tune. Many months later, in my search for the reason why I had to keep repeating this instruction, I found out the cause. I asked her a simple question:

"Is there anything stopping you from stretching?"

"I am frightened my skin is going to crack when I stretch" she replied.

Only then did I find out that she had dry skin, which would cause a lot of pain. We tapped a sequence for this fear. Most importantly, Tracey now knew that she could tell me if her hands were bothering her when she was playing the cello and she could take a break if required.

Her intonation improved. She became more confident and was now able to take her Grade 1 cello exam, which she passed with distinction. Tracey was very proud of herself; she had not thought she would get such a high mark. As for me, I can only say that, as I was accompanying her on the piano and enjoying her performance, a tear came to my eye as I thought of all she had come through to play so well.

There was another remarkable aspect to Tracey's case. One day she told me that she had helped a friend who was having period pains, guiding her through the TFT *collarbone breathing* procedure (see Appendix).

It was not the first time one of my students, having so effectively used TFT for musical performance, had helped their fellow classmates, particularly for exam nerves. One student had used TFT so successfully for musical performance, that one summer's day they got their friends tapping in class. The teacher, upon hearing the humming - during the nine gamut procedure - thought there was a bee in the classroom! When the cause was identified, my student was invited to give a demonstration. The class teacher, who does 'brain gym' with her class, now uses TFT as one of her strategies to help prepare the children for exams.

The wonderful thing about having used TFT with my students and colleagues is how they now use these techniques in their everyday life, not just for musical performance. One student told me:

"The helicopter flight was an awful experience. I used the tapping to stop me being sick."

Which sequence did you use? I asked them.

"The PR spot, side of hand. It was all I had room for!"

Chapter 24
Tapping out the tension

This article, written by my piano student Sarah Taylor, was published in Music Teacher magazine in August 2008. In it she describes how the empathetic approach of her teacher and the use of TFT tapping, helped her overcome a mid-life performance crisis.

As Sarah recalled, "Having encouraged my daughter to sit her clarinet exams right through to Grade 7, I never really gave a second thought to what I now know is the terrifying ordeal of a performance under exam conditions. My own recent experience has left me with great admiration for the thousands of children and adults who are subjected to this ruthless process every year."

"A bit of a late starter, I took up the piano at the ripe old age of forty-five and was delighted when I received a merit for my Grade 1 exam. Eighteen months later I sat my Grade 3 piano exam, having diligently practised my scales and pieces. Just minutes into the exam, however, I found myself quivering like a leaf and staring blankly at the music, which was suddenly indecipherable. My heart was racing and I was literally all fingers and thumbs. I couldn't understand it. I had practised endlessly, knew the pieces off by heart and had felt reasonably confident that morning. What was happening? I struggled through the exam, close to tears, and then ran out of the room apologising to the examiner."

"Unsurprisingly, I failed. I was devastated. A normally confident and articulate adult, I was used to making presentations and had even sung *a cappella* in front of an audience. I was not, however, used to feeling overwhelmed with panic and unable to perform. My confidence was badly shaken and I wasn't even sure I wanted to continue with my piano lessons. I sought advice from a number of musicians and my daughter's clarinet teacher suggested I contact Rosemary Wiseman, a piano teacher who helps people with performance anxiety."

"I wasn't sure what to expect when I went to Rosemary's Edgware home for my first lesson. She had asked me to come 'au naturel' - devoid of any cosmetics, deodorant or perfume. We spent the first half an hour discussing my feelings about the exam and playing for her for the first time. It was an enormous relief to speak to someone who understood what I had been through and who wanted to help me. Rosemary introduced me to the principles of Thought Field Therapy (TFT) and gave me some simple tapping exercises to use when I was feeling anxious or stressed. She also explained that chemicals in cosmetics or even diet could cause psychological reversal and interfere with memory and concentration."

"I must admit, I was a little sceptical at first. It almost seemed too simple and a bit 'New Agey'. But I was so desperate to conquer this crippling anxiety that I was willing to give it a go.

"Rosemary helped me to understand that my fear of failure had become an emotional block, which was actually preventing me from performing well – a self-fulfilling prophecy. As I tapped different points on my body, I concentrated on the source of my stress, and gradually the anxiety seemed to subside. I felt calmer, more in control and more focused. The tapping exercises helped me to reduce the fear to a more manageable level, which allowed me to continue with the performance."

"For the next few weeks Rosemary took me through my Grade 3 pieces, incorporating the tapping routines whenever my performance anxiety returned and giving me lots of practical tips about coping with the exam situation, such as remembering to breathe! She also encouraged me to perform for friends and family whenever possible using the TFT tapping to control my nerves. Each time I performed I realised that it wasn't a complete disaster if I made a mistake or two. The important thing was to keep going and the tapping allowed me to do that."

"When the big day arrived, I felt reasonably calm. I turned up at the exam centre in plenty of time and ran through some TFT exercises. As I entered the exam room I felt my old fears returning but, having handed the examiner a list of my pieces, I spent a few seconds tapping as he made notes. Like many students in exam conditions, I did not give my best performance that day and the nerves were still very much in evidence. But this time I was able to use the tapping techniques to regain control of myself at various points in the exam, to focus on what I was doing and, most importantly, to keep going. This in itself was a great achievement and a few weeks later I was delighted to hear that I had passed with a very respectable mark. Not only have I proved to myself that I can play the piano at this level, I have also learned that a previously crippling anxiety can be reduced by this incredibly simple technique."

Chapter 25
Tip toes

If, after reading Sarah Taylor's case, you are still wondering what happens if the examiner sees me tapping, read on.

There was just one question the parent of this exam candidate did not ask their child as they were preparing everything they could possibly think of prior to them entering the exam room.

I was asked to accompany James, aged twelve. His father had entered him for Grade 4 violin. It would have meant rehearsing with him just two days before his exam and he was also due to take his Grade 4 piano exam later that week. There were concerns about his level of preparation for both exams. Fortunately, after speaking to his violin teacher - a professor at The Royal Academy of Music - the violin exam was rearranged for a Special Visit a few weeks later, allowing me some time to work with him.

James had rhythmic and intonation problems and due to lack of communications, no aural practice had been done apart from that in his actual Grade 4 piano exam. It was only after getting to know him better that I found many of his issues were about anxiety and the right kind of practice, rather than just lack of it.

After tapping a TFT sequence for general anxiety James said, "I feel more positive. My mind is cleared of everything." We also tapped for anxiety about the exam getting closer, the lack of preparation and performing to me; "It is not bothering me anymore. I am happy, as I know the solution that can get me ready." We used *sing play* to improve the intonation. There was a remarkable change in his violin playing following these techniques. We also tapped for pain in his right arm after which he said, "My arm didn't hurt. I forgot about it, literally. I feel so happy." After tapping for the embarrassment of singing to someone in the aural tests, his singing improved. It was wonderful to see him so happy, as a calm and confident James began to emerge.

Violin exam day

The start time was delayed by twenty minutes. As I was about to enter the exam room with James, the homeowner of the Special Visit centre asked me if I had a music stand which I obviously did not have and neither did he. As a solution was sought, the exam was delayed further. I quickly improvised and used an object that was leaning against the wall as a stand. In this position, James was unable to see me at the piano.

After the third piece, I saw he was crying and breathing rapidly. I quickly guided him through a TFT *tapping sequence for trauma* and then established that he feared he would fail his exam. It was the first time that I had ever needed to treat a candidate in the exam room itself. I was grateful to the examiner, who was reassuring and allowed me to stay in the room for a few minutes to help James rapidly calm down enough to continue his exam.

We were fortunate that the examiner had a relaxed, positive and calming manner at all times, from the moment of entering the exam room to leaving it. He gave us the feeling that there was time to sort things out, even though he was clearly aware they were running late.

James described his exam experience to me:

"When I realised I did not have a music stand my heart started racing. What am I going to do? I started panicking that it might make me fail. I am not used to it and had to play on *tip toes* to see the music as it was so high. I felt like crying all the way through my pieces. I know I could have played better. It was humiliating and I didn't want to continue. I could have been 'that boy in the street' (see Chapter 1)."

"For the aural my voice couldn't sing. You can't think when you are upset.

The scales did not go well. In the middle I was asked to play E major and I did not know if it was a scale or an arpeggio I was supposed to be playing."

After his exam James went home feeling all right, which is quite something after what he had been through. He was keen to share his experiences in the hope that it may help others.

James was delighted to pass both his piano and violin exams and can now take future music exams with confidence.

Chapter 26
Music to my ears

Let us consider the case of thirteen-year-old Grade 8 violin candidate, Amy. She has already passed her Grade 8 piano and Grade 7 singing with distinction and plays the saxophone for fun. I am her performance coach and accompanist.

Her 'extremely supportive' mother is upset, as this time Amy has been entered too early by her new school violin teacher. She has one violin teacher in school and another at home, an arrangement that has worked well in the past for her and her sibling. This is what makes this case so remarkable; there are few people who could cope with such a situation. Teachers are individual, having different styles and techniques. We can benefit from this variety. However, having this happen simultaneously could be confusing to both student and teacher.

Amy does not like two of her three pieces, nor the violin any more. I am doing everything possible to get her to enjoy the music, yet it is still not working. With just four days to go to the exam and searching for something that can help, I ask her if she likes her violin teachers. Amy tells me that she does not like the one at school, as she is negative about her and her playing. This had started when this teacher found a *time saver* on the music and realised there was another teacher involved. Once again, it shows that we as teachers, whatever the circumstances, need to keep a positive approach to students.

In seconds I guide Amy through tapping the PR spot, side of hand, for this negativity. I also use an NLP technique as we reduce the image of that teacher to a dot and she stamps her foot on it. Her playing immediately transforms – she is playing 'music' – as she finds freedom to express herself.

I record our rehearsal and discover – through *Zoom* – that there are just a few notes and rhythms that the two violin teachers have not noticed Amy is playing incorrectly. As we work on improving the pieces, I recall the distinction she got for her last grade. I know she will make it in four days time and that somehow I will too. In the past, her mother would often say that her high marks were not high enough. This one is different. They will both be happy for just a pass.

It is a challenging accompaniment and we need to perform as a 'duo'. The challenge also involves making time to practise. I keep my *Weekly Rhythm Record* to keep me on track. Having accompanied Amy for most of her other grades, I feel committed to supporting her for her final grade. I seem to have an inbuilt 'keep calm' mantra as I utilise *Zoom88* for us both as exam day approaches. "*Say play* is useful," Amy comments as we progress further.

It is the day before the exam. Despite all, Amy is still not enjoying two of her pieces or liking the violin any better. She is ready to go on to the viola, as it has a lower sound, or even the oboe.

There is a massive traffic problem, causing many of the children to be late for the school where the exam is to take place today. I am stuck in it. With the use of my sense of direction and husband Laurence acting as a sat nav, by looking at a map, I am shocked to discover I have arrived at the school on time. A short TFT tapping sequence to recover quickly and calm myself from the, "what if...I could not have found a way out of that jam?" is welcome as we are about to go into the exam room some minutes early. Amy taps a short sequence to reduce some excitement that was showing itself as nerves.

Apart from the first page turn, all goes well and my fingers seem to be playing themselves. A thought comes into my mind – "How will I get home? Let's sort that one out later," I say to myself. I am so wrapped up in the music I completely forget about the examiner. Out of the corner of my eyes I observe Amy is swaying to the music, something I have hardly seen in the rehearsals.

After the exam she is smiling broadly and looks relieved as she tells me, "I enjoyed it and I liked the pieces." "And the violin?" I ask expectantly. "It's OK" she replies, as if she has become reacquainted with an old friend. My response is immediate, "This is music to my ears, you have made my day!"

The result at this point seems secondary. Eleven days later I get a text from Amy: "Thank you for all of your work. I GOT A DISTINCTION yay."

I also received this email from Amy's mother:
"Amy had her first exploratory lesson on the viola last week. I am really proud of the fact that she has achieved a high mark. I would have been extremely happy with a pass, based on the time constraints and her falling out of love with the instrument. Really pleased that her confidence in herself is restored and she can now move on to playing pieces that she really likes. I must say though, that she could not have achieved this without the efforts of all three teachers, including yourself."

Chapter 27
Finger biter to finger tapper

With kind permission of his wife Mary, one of the more unusual cases I will share with you is that of Justin Jones. He came to see me, when he was fifty-four, for help with his habit of picking and nibbling his fingers, rather than for help with musical performance. I found out during the consultation that he played violin in one of the major London symphony orchestras. In the past he had *"tried hypnotherapy, but not with any success,"* although he did find it relaxing.

Justin, who described himself as a secret nibbler, was experiencing some stress and trauma. He also lacked energy. After guiding him through a TFT tapping sequence for a strong urge to pick his fingers, he no longer had the urge and felt more alert. He also got benefit from tapping for other issues and was able to feel calm after releasing some trauma about a loved one who had passed away.

During his follow-up session he told me that his nail-biting problem had been 'sorted'. His positive comments about the benefit of his treatment were of special interest to musicians: he felt more relaxed playing his violin when performing. He found the tapping helped him far more than the Alexander Technique, which he had been using previously. He now naturally shifted his posture on stage to achieve a more flexible balance. Justin was so impressed with the tapping techniques that he thought I should contact the person in charge of health and well being in professional orchestras.

He now had just one concern and that was a fear of his bow shaking on the strings, something he did not want to be noticed doing. Again, with a tapping sequence for anxiety, this fear immediately disappeared.

By chance on 9th December 2007, Laurence and I attended a concert at the Royal Festival Hall where we saw Justin perform with the Philharmonia Orchestra and observed that the shaking had gone. We enjoyed a drink with him during the interval. It is not always possible to follow up a client like this.

At the time of writing, I found out that Justin had passed away from terminal cancer. He was fifty-nine years old. Apparently he used to call me *Dr Finger biter*. It is Mary's wish that sharing her late husband's case will help others in the music profession.

Chapter 28
From knuckles to chuckles

The way that forty-eight-year-old Jayne and I met is, once again, a story of my caring for wildlife. I had found an injured bird in our local park and contacted a wildlife rescue group. They put me in touch with Jayne, one of the volunteers, who collected the young bird and took it to their centre.

I knew TFT tapping had enabled me to pick up and rescue the bird. I messaged Jayne to let her know this, in case it could help others to rescue wildlife. What I was about to find out was that it would help Jayne herself, when she subsequently booked an appointment and became my client.

She initially wanted help with anxiety, panic attacks and blockages to move on. Some months later she wanted help with a past trauma that had still been bothering her since she was a teenager. Her piano teacher had been impatient with her. To make matters worse, her parents focused their attention on her brother, who was gifted. While her sibling went on to have a successful musical career, Jayne had been left traumatised.

Her brother had not liked Mrs 'X' much, he told Jayne recently to her surprise. Even though she never hit his fingers, he never really enjoyed the lessons and only achieved Grade 2. He had another teacher after, yet did not flourish until he had lessons from a famous teacher and achieved Grade 8 distinction some years later. He stayed in touch with this teacher until she died.

Jayne described her transformational experience in an email sent to me in November 2016:

"When I was about five, I had a piano teacher called Mrs 'X'. She taught my brother first and had preference over him to me. I found it difficult to co-ordinate my fingers and read music fully.

I didn't thoroughly learn to read books until I was six and then I was one of the best and fastest readers in the class for several years. If I played a wrong note, Mrs 'X' would hit my fingers. I hated this, but never told her.

I practiced in between lessons, but dreaded each one. I think Mrs 'X' may even have mentioned how good my brother was and how I wasn't very good, which made me feel quite hurt and untalented. I was pleased when the lessons stopped.

It obviously upset me until now, so when I broke down in one of your sessions, it was because it all came back very vividly. Through the tapping technique you used with me several times, I felt the pain and sadness lift. I could view the event much more as an observer. Since then I don't feel the same about the memory. I feel much more detached and no longer experience the extreme hurt. So thanks a lot for that." ☺

Chapter 29
"With music lessons my world switches."

My piano student Claire, aged sixty-seven, was not performing her Grade 1 standard pieces as well as she could. She appeared stressed and frustrated and told me, as she held her hand over the right side of her head, that she could not stop thinking about a traumatic incident which had occurred earlier that day.

She had gone for a blood pressure test on this snowy morning and had trouble parking. Consequently, she only had ten minutes to wait before her appointment, instead of the usual half an hour. As always, she saw straight through the nurse's calming words. Her usual methods to calm herself were not enough on this occasion and due to the high reading of her blood pressure, a twenty-four-hour blood pressure monitor test was suggested. She decided she would go ahead with this test, even though she knew she did not have high blood pressure. It was also suggested that she consider some help for her anxiety.

Claire is one student who generally does not feel comfortable about using TFT tapping. I therefore suggested that I introduce her to another technique that I had learned from its developer, my hypnotherapy trainer, Stephen Brooks, which only involves the use of a few words.

Claire, to my surprise, was open to me using this with her. I had once before tested out the words of Non Attachment Therapy (NAT) with her, using them once only, as a passing suggestion, just to ensure that she reacted positively, which she had.

Her SUD (Subjective Units of Distress) was 8. After repeating a 'round' of the NAT words '*This Brain is having a thought*' several times aloud, then several more in her head, she said, "It changes your head space." Her SUD had reduced to a 4. After a few more repetitions of the words she was now on 0.5 and told me that she felt more relaxed. Her performance improved and she was now calm and even amused by any small errors.

Claire said she would be interested to use NAT when she takes her blood pressure next.

Travel problems caused by snow had been unpredictable on this day of her piano lesson. It had been uncertain whether she would manage to attend. She texted me afterwards with a simple message: 'I am glad I made it to you today.'

Chapter 30
"The nutter in the back row"

In February 2005, I obtained several tickets to be part of the studio audience during a recording of *"Who Wants To Be A Millionaire?"* at the Elstree Film Studios, Borehamwood. This popular television quiz show offered a maximum cash prize of one million pounds for correctly answering successive multiple-choice questions of increasing (or, in some cases, random) difficulty. Its host was Chris Tarrant.

I was seated in the back row. Everything appeared to be going smoothly until Chris Tarrant embraced a particular contestant, who was doing extremely well. The recording was stopped so that the makeup artist could come out and apply a dry-cleaning solution to Chris's suit jacket, in order to remove make up that had gone onto it from the contestant.

In his inimitable style, Chris joked about the smell, sniffing the arm of his jacket and telling the audience, "It's gone right to my head!" He even invited them to join in the sniffing.

When Chris tried to continue filming, he found it impossible to speak, almost as if he was 'tongue-tied'. The camera crew had to do several 'retakes', in between which Chris sniffed his jacket and joked with the audience to hide his embarrassment over his speech problem.

From my position in the back row of the audience, Chris's problem was obvious. He had inhaled a powerful individual energy toxin and had immediately gone into Psychological Reversal! (See Chapter 12)

I sent my business card down to him with a message to stop sniffing his suit and to tap the PR spot on the side of his hand. He read it aloud to the audience and then asked me to identify myself. Standing up, I explained the method behind the apparent madness and demonstrated to him exactly what to do, all the way from the back row! I also demonstrated the anxiety algorithm (sequence). When Chris asked me what it is that I do to help people, I told the audience it was Thought Field Therapy.

Chris then rechristened it "Thought Pit Therapy" as he had just tapped under his armpit! The warm up artist meanwhile was also very interested and wanted to know exactly what the therapy was called. So while the comedy went on I was able to point out its correct title.

Exposing his lack of belief that this could possibly work and perhaps his state of psychological reversal, Chris said "but I can't do this while they are filming!".

As I was almost sucked into his state of disbelief myself, I was about to give him some further instruction when I recalled that the only evidence for a practitioner that our treatment has worked is when we are able to observe or are told by the client that the problem presented has gone. Chris had not said that this was the case.

At this point the floor manager became concerned that we were taking up too much time, "We have a show to get on with!", he called out. In reality and unknown to us all at that moment, the tapping advice SAVED time.

I have come across this comment before when using TFT for performance enhancement. The onlooker believes it is time wasted; yet what follows is a great saving of time. Less effort has to be put in afterwards and this leads to far less anxiety and frustration as well as improved performance.

And so the "nutter that they save the seat for in the back row" was silenced and the show went on. Interestingly and perhaps not unexpectedly, Chris Tarrant had no further speech problems and no further retakes were necessary.

I have since been told that Chris has my card stuck up in his dressing room and he has kindly issued the following statement:

"It was extraordinary! Whatever the cleaning fluid was that they sprayed onto my jacket, it was clearly giving me problems. My eyes were pouring fluid and I was really struggling to keep recording the show. Rosemary recognised the symptoms straight away and sorted me out there and then in front of the audience and in no time at all. It was amazing."

Finally, a big thank you to those members of my family who were sitting next to "the nutter in the back row" at the time and allowed me to be unstoppable in sending that message down to Chris Tarrant.

TFT and Speech-making

Alongside Chris Tarrant's testimonial, I should like to quote that of Marion:

"I contacted Rosemary when I was due to make a presentation to a conference audience of over five thousand people. Although I knew my material very well, the thought of speaking in front of that many people was a very daunting prospect."

"Rosemary very quickly showed me some simple techniques to help me cope with the stress of the big day – both in the run up to the event, and also on the day itself. At first, when she explained to me the tapping sequences, it all seemed too simple to be true. However, I went through the sequences a number of times, and particularly on the day itself, to great effect. The results were virtually immediate and I am sure they went a long way to making me feel very confident in my own abilities."

"After the event I was complimented by many people about how calm and confident I appeared, which I am sure was in no small part due to the TFT processes that I had used."

This is what Marion wrote to her team after the event:

"Firstly I want to say thank you to everyone who has been kind enough to give me such positive feedback on my presentation on Saturday - I was completely terrified and it was great that so many of you were there to cheer me on and have taken the time to pass on your feedback since. Thank you - and all I can say is make sure you get the chance to speak at the national conference - it has made me so fired up as a result!"

Chapter 31
A head-turning case

My piano student Tammy, aged eight, was stuck on *A Carol for Christmas - We Three Kings*. She kept making 'mistakes', as she was confusing the use of her left and right hands (see R for Reversals, Chapter 12).

At one point, she attempted to turn her head 'upside down' in her effort to read the music and answer my simple question, "How do you know that note is an F?" Her explanation was logical, though incorrect; G in the bass clef was to her an F in the treble clef.

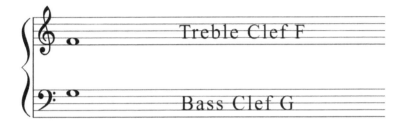

When these issues continued for some weeks, I knew that something was interfering with her performance. I spoke to Tammy's mother and discovered that the family had plug-in air fresheners in every room of their home. I suggested these be removed.

The following week Tammy's piano playing was fine. She concentrated well, corrected herself if there was a mistake and progressed on in her tutor book. Her father, whose headaches had also ceased, clarified at the end of the lesson that the air fresheners had been turned off and not removed. Even this had made a huge difference. For some weeks things went well.

Significantly, after a school holiday, Tammy's problems reoccurred. *The Musical Alphabet* from Me and My Piano Part 2 sounded nothing like the piece. I knew this was temporary. Her parents told me that they had turned the air fresheners back on again over the holiday. I guided Tammy with a TFT tapping procedure to neutralise the effect of the air fresheners so the lesson was more productive.

The following week her playing was back to normal. With air fresheners now completely removed, Tammy continued to progress well.

Chapter 32
Recovery by flute, piano, singing…and tapping
Josie, my Mum's story

Some dates and events are very memorable. We may remember exactly where we were, or exactly what we were doing when they happened. This applies equally to weddings or world events and for weather conditions ranging from a snowstorm to an exceptionally windy day.

I can remember exactly what I was doing just before my 88 year-old mother Josie had a dense stroke.

It was 6th November 2009. My sister Marilynne was away in Israel, so she did not give our mum her daily early morning call as she had been doing recently.

I was at home getting ready to take Josie to a 9.50 am nurse's appointment at her local GP surgery to get her arm injury dressed from a TIA mini stroke she had had some weeks earlier. Although I had called her, she had not picked up the phone. Then my brother Bernard rang to let me know that our Mum had been sick the previous evening. His call saved her life, and prevented further brain injury, as it set alarm bells ringing for me.

I fled from my house, without telling my husband Laurence where I was going. I was at Mum's flat within five minutes. Not knowing if she was alive, I called out into the silence of the flat. Suddenly I heard a groan coming from the floor to the side of her bed.....she reached up to me with her left arm and held my hand. Then she fell silent and was unable to speak.

I immediately realised that she had suffered a stroke or "brain attack". While waiting for the ambulance, I immediately began tapping the psychological reversal (PR) spot on the side of her hand. I also did the collarbone breathing for her (see Appendix).

Although very sceptical at first, Josie had become a keen 'tapper' and had used TFT techniques for a number of issues very successfully in the past. Now and for some time, I was to use 'surrogate tapping' methods.

On examination at A & E (Accident and Emergency) Barnet General, they observed that Josie's right leg and arm could not move and she was unable to swallow. She had experienced a 'left hemisphere' stroke.

Soon after, she was admitted to Spruce Ward, which is a specialist acute stroke unit at Barnet Hospital.

For her whole family, there was a lot to learn. Stroke recovery and rehabilitation journeys are different for every person. For our family and the medical staff, this meant that we had to live from day to day and all strive for the best possible outcome.

Apart from the useful booklets and documents published by The Stroke Association, I read the book *'My Year off' - Rediscovering Life After A Stroke* by Robert McCrum, which I found helpful, especially as it outlined how acupuncture had helped his recovery.

I also watched the film of a book I had read some years earlier to my dad when he had Progressive Supranuclear Palsy (PSP) and when there was little else he could do in terms of communication: *The Diving Bell and the Butterfly* was written by Jean-Dominique Bauby after he had suffered a massive stroke.

My ongoing work and previous experience with my client, May O'Donnell, who had suffered a similar stroke to my mother, certainly assisted me in helping her. May, her son and medical and nursing staff, (at the same hospitals as Josie), had given me feedback and encouragement about how the work I was doing had helped.

I particularly remember the day I visited May in the weeks after she had her stroke. I did some tapping and then played the flute to her. After I left, I was told she suddenly started to wave to other patients on the ward.

Her son wrote to me: *"You did a very good job, May is always happier after your visits. The staff are impressed as well."*

As a hypnotherapist, TFT diagnostic practitioner and professional musician, I was certainly glad of all the skills I had acquired, as staying positive and keeping one's energy up were all important in the daily hospital visits to Josie that we made for many months.

As there were usually no emotional issues with Josie, for six months I treated her with TFT for any infections, visualising positive outcomes and treating reversals for general recovery on a mostly daily basis, then gradually and naturally decreasing as she improved.

Often TFT practitioners, when discussing treatment, will ask colleagues, "Which tapping sequences (Algorithms) did you use?"

and "How did you know what to tap for?" I used the nine gamut procedure, reversal treatments - psychological reversal (PR) spot, under nose and collarbone breathing regularly. In time, with guidance, Josie was able to carry out the visualisation sequence and the nine gamut procedure by herself. It was interesting to observe how she managed to complete it depending on her condition.

Whenever I used tapping for her stroke recovery, I looked for signs that Josie was happy for me to use it. One day I asked her directly if she felt the tapping helped. She said "everything helps". Of course her personality and a positive disposition helped enormously, as well as the prayers, healing and love and care of the family, friends and medical staff.

Sometimes I have been asked if I am a 'Music Therapist'. Being a musician, I have found ways to use music therapeutically with some clients. With Josie we did a lot of singing and sometimes I played the flute to her. (I was glad I had learned at least one portable instrument!) Josie would join in vocally, or move in time to the music. This was a good way to communicate and it helped in a therapeutic way with her speech. It also showed me how much life was still in her.

In the early days of her recovery, even before she could speak, Josie became known on the ward for her humming. She sang along with me *in tune*. This was particularly interesting, as Josie was my first 'client' who I had helped to sing in tune after many years of silence during communal singing.

One day, although at first she had no speech, after I played the flute to her, she suddenly said "very nice" then began to say a few more words.

In January 2010 my sister Marilynne told me "You can be an 'ordinary' daughter today, you don't need to tap her every day" as by this time Josie's speech was much improved.

In one short phone call, Josie remarked "I'm jogging along slowly'. We then began regularly singing an American folk-song '*Jim along* (meaning jog along) *Josie*'.

Hey, jim along, jim along Josie,
Hey, jim along, jim along Jo.
Hey, jim along, jim along Josie,
Hey, jim along, jim along Jo.

As a family, we kept a diary during Josie's rehabilitation. This helped with communications between us, as changes in her condition were rapid. In time, as she began to recover - and for the rest of her life - Josie took pride in this diary and made sure we all completed it daily.

On 23rd December 2009 there was another one of those events that I can remember clearly. As I later wrote to a friend:

"What a journey this is! Yesterday when I went to see Mum they asked me to go and have 'a coffee' while they did some new physio. I found myself at the hospital Christmas Carol service. The lady who was supposed to be leading the singing could not attend as she had a cold. It was being recorded for transmission to all Barnet hospitals on Christmas Day and it immediately became obvious they needed leading, so I stepped in."

Father Tom Baron, the Barnet Hospital Chaplain, asked me afterwards which Church I attended. Obviously he was impressed that I knew so many Carols. Once I had explained that I was Jewish, he told me about their Jewish chaplain, Rabbi Yisroel Fine and the Jewish volunteers who could visit Mum. Now that gave her something to think about.

Josie's speedy recovery amazed both our family and medics alike. On one occasion the Consultant was about to administer, within earshot of her, an 'end of life care package'. In early February, she had suffered yet another and most serious bout of pneumonia. This was probably caused by Norovirus and being unable to swallow at the time. Josie soon made that consultant aware that she was not yet ready to 'go'.

She fought hard and described her experience, at one point, as 'a fast moving soap opera.' When one of her eleven grandchildren once asked her why she was a fighter, she replied "Because I have a lot to fight for".

I really noticed how much Josie was striving to get better when she did the exercises for the Speech and Language Therapists (SALT) team. Although she was well motivated, which certainly helped, the exercises themselves were quite difficult to do. For example, Josie and the bed had to be in a special position, which required considerable effort on her part.

One day a member of the SALT team had to inform us the video - fluoroscopy had revealed Josie was still unable to swallow safely, making clear that the exercises and the TFT tapping had so far not worked. However, they suggested that she still continued doing the exercises. Even while the SALT member was saying this, I noticed how Josie was already practising the exercises. Her reaction was clear.

In contrast, the non-invasive TFT procedures were easy to administer. So, following the perseverance of the medical team, we continued with the tapping.

I also did a Hypnosis session with Josie, taking suggestions for stroke patient rehabilitation from the D. Corydon Hammond's *Handbook of Hypnotic suggestions and metaphors.*

Treatments by the physiotherapists were also extremely important. By the end of April 2010, we were invited to watch Josie doing her physio; I saw my mum walk along the hospital corridor for the first time since she had her stroke. It was a very moving experience. Words were not enough. The physio told me, "We don't get many people like your mum."

Throughout her recovery Josie remained determined as ever. Still, in November 2009 it was a brave decision for her to agree to have a Percutaneous Endoscopic Gastrostomy (PEG) feeding tube fitted. It would replace the nasal gastric tube, which she had done very well to keep in for so long. This was also a life-making decision for her. Wearing that PEG for six months gave her time to recover. Mum's calm nature, co-operation, motivation and strength were already evident to the medical staff and this surely helped them with their treatment for her.

By now Josie had made sufficient progress to continue her rehabilitation at Finchley Memorial Hospital, on the George Brunskill Ward, which specialises in Stroke Rehabilitation. The staff there suggested that I bring in a keyboard for Mum. Prior to her stroke, playing the piano was one of her great loves. (She had passed Grade 2 piano in 2008, aged eighty-six.) Not long after this we had a family singsong. Her diary entry for that day says it all: "*Grandma is clapping!* and she managed to play the keyboard...C major scale, yes, with *each* hand!".

After only six months in hospital, Josie could walk with a frame, write and play the piano a little, speak reasonably well and eat and drink normally.

When she was discharged, the staff at Finchley Memorial Hospital wrote an entry in her diary "*Dearest Josephine all the Nursing Staff are so proud of the way you have progressed whilst on*

George Brunskill Ward. We all wish you well for the future. You have showed courage and determination. Truly a superstar!"

In May 2010 my mother was admitted to Hill House Care Home, in Elstree, where her late husband Sam had stayed some years previously. Once again, she was "open to visitors". She described it as "home from home". Within weeks Josie was eating in the dining room and joining in various activities such as quizzes, art and keep fit, as well as playing her piano. She insisted on sitting *exactly* in the middle of the piano. She also read from sheet music as she played along on the keyboard with another lady from the home as part of a keyboard lesson.

These last nine months were an incredible journey for us all. We learned so much about human strength, love, friendship and about positive attitude.

More recently Josie had made even greater strides in her recovery. In January 2014, she performed the piano for her Life After Stroke Award, an achievement filmed by my son David. While preparing for this, she realised how she could use musical notation to assist her playing even better than she had thought possible just after her stroke. She even progressed from sitting in her wheelchair to sitting on the piano stool.

Before her stroke, Josie's hands would tremble when performing in concerts or in front of groups of people. So although she had intended that her son Bernard visit her later in the day after the performance, I became concerned when, unannounced, he arrived with his daughter Joanna and her boyfriend. Despite this, Josie ended up performing live to an audience of the five of us.

She both announced and played her own composition *'Walking in the Snow'*, and then *'Lightly Row'* a folk song from Me and My Piano part 2. It went amazingly well, with her steady hands and calm approach. It was certainly the best that she had performed to an audience, even before her stroke.

Our mum's recovery would not have been possible if she had not received help and encouragement from the medical staff at Barnet and Finchley Memorial Hospitals, Hill House, from Roger and Joanne Callahan, Dr Colin Barron and of course to all family and friends who contributed in various ways. Thank you all.

Josie continued to play the piano and enjoy music until she passed away peacefully in May 2018.

Chapter 33
From typing to tapping…..
(Published in the Thought Field May 2015)

It began back in the 1980s. We were living in North London. My wife Alex was receiving cello lessons from Rosemary Wiseman. One spring day in 1985, Rosemary and her husband Laurence invited us to lunch with them. Knowing that I wrote books and magazine articles, they mentioned that they had an ageing grandmother, in her nineties, with many personal memories of the family. Would I be interested in interviewing Bessie Marks with a view to "ghosting" her autobiography?

As I was a little busy with another book at the time, I had suggested they buy a tape-recorder and get their respected relative to dictate her memories. Some months later, Rosemary told me that they now had some twenty "Granny Tapes". I then suggested they employ a secretary to transcribe them and sort them into decades – the 1930s, the 1950s etc. Some months later, they told me that this had been done and then looked at me intently.

I only met Bessie Marks once, but during the next few months, I attempted to step into the mind of a Jewish woman who had suffered a great deal in her life and wrote up her story. Once finished, we found a printer and presented him with the manuscript and family photos of what we had called 'An Open Mind' פתוח ראש (Psalm 119, 99 "I have learned the lessons of life from many sources" - The Autobiography of Bessie Marks (née Meek)." Based on the "Granny Tapes".

The slim dark blue volume of only 157 pages was just being bound when Bessie died in June 1988. I was invited to attend her stone setting. Wearing a kippah and standing among the other men, I must have been one of the only goyim in the prayer hall. When the rabbi said "Bessie Marks is no longer, but we have something unique and very special to remember her by, thanks to our friend Kevin," I was very touched. At the reception afterwards, I autographed books for members of the family and they autographed my copy. It really should have been Bessie who did the signing.

In 1992, Alex and I, with our two children, left England and took up residence in a small village outside Bordeaux in Southern France, where we have been ever since. Inevitably, we lost contact with many people whom we had known in London; including Rosemary and Laurence.

Then one day I received an email from Rosemary inviting me to help her write her own book. In our subsequent phone call, she told me that writing a book had been a childhood ambition. She had been toying with it for some years, making notes and doing doodles. Recalling her granny's autobiography, she thought of me again. But where was I? Thanks to social networking, we were soon in touch. We started at the beginning of 2014.

I must confess that when I first heard about TFT, it seemed a somewhat simplistic way to eliminate traumas and pains. But one day, with Rosemary's notes and watching a YouTube demonstration by Dr Mary Cowley, I decided to try it out on my own anxiety. I should explain that, since the 1960s, I had been subject to bouts of depression – for which I had been prescribed medications – Librium, Prozac etc. and anti-anxiety and sleeping pills.

To my surprise, tapping had eliminated my anxiety in less than ten minutes! Following guidance via 'live' Skype by Rosemary, I tried it out on others problems, only to find them disappearing, one by one, like the skins of an onion. To mention a few – my recurring fear of rejection going back to my childhood; my fear (at over sixty) of death; my fear of the doctor's and dentist's surgery; my fear as a writer of not meeting my deadlines; my impatience; I even found that I had anxiety about the absence of a longstanding anxiety. I tapped for this and it too disappeared!

Perhaps most relevant to Rosemary's book is that I sing tenor in an amateur choir here in Bordeaux, taking on such technical challenges as the Brahms 'German Requiem' and Dvorak's 'Stabat Mater'. To my delight I discovered that tapping has helped with eliminating any anxieties I may have had over the difficulties of these works, either in choir practice or before a performance.

Once I realised that I could eliminate any anxiety with TFT, I felt I had to share it with my friends. This is where I learned that some people resist TFT. Firstly, I discovered how some individuals do not want to let go of their anxieties, believing that these are part of their identity. Secondly, many people feel that they must pay to be healed and that a system that is free, simply cannot work. But then were not the wise words spoken by the Prophets initially free for all?

In any religion, is the donation of money a way to Heaven? Look at the larger mosques and temples and cathedrals. To approach the Divinity, during one's brief lifetime on this beautiful Planet, must one really follow the paths of suffering – from daily confession of sins to the painful extremes of self-harming? TFT says that suffering is not necessary for a full life. Arguably is not TFT another gift from God?

Dany had been looking after her aged mother round the clock. I showed her a TFT algorithm; She told me that her SUD was 11. We did a couple of holons and PR correction on the side of her hand. When I asked her about her SUD she would not tell me, but smiled and admitted that "ce n'est plus à onze!" = it's no longer 11!

Dominique sings solo in her local choirs and also teaches English. When she came to visit us, she was impressed by the change in my behaviour – calmer and more positive. I introduced her to TFT. Several weeks later she emailed me "Kevin, Marion and I tried the tapping thing. Sometimes it works, sure it soothes us most of the time, but we still can't sleep well when we're too stressed. We have to work on it still. Thanks a lot anyway."

Gordon, my sixty-year-old bachelor friend, has a long history of psychological problems. I sent him emails and YouTube links. He is gradually learning how it helps.

Michelle visited us, the day her father died. She was anxious about her extreme feelings during the funeral service. We tapped – and her SUD lowered from 8 to 2. When I asked her how it went, she said "sans inquietude" = without anxiety.

But back to this remarkable book. Encouraged by her family, particularly her mother Josie, her patient husband Laurence and her IT adviser son David, Rosemary began to write and under my supervision, painstakingly revised each paragraph of this book: *Zoom88*. Yes, we have had our DLW (delete last word) literary problems; tapping has even helped that as well! In all, the writing of this book has taken us four years.

As a historian and sometimes fiction writer, I have often wondered what the History of the World might have been if tapping had been discovered and passed on by ancient civilisations. What art might have been if suffering composers such as Chopin, and painters such as Van Gogh had been able to tap; maybe your readers can inform me about this!

Just to say that it has been a pleasure working with Rosemary on this book and I join her in hoping that all those music teachers, students and performers around the world who read it will derive full positive benefit from it. Thank you Rosemary. Thank you Roger.

Kevin Desmond
desmond.book@wanadoo.fr
Bordeaux, FRANCE

Chapter 34
The man who developed TFT

My book would not be complete without a tribute to the man who developed TFT. Roger Jerry Callahan (1925-2013) was a successful clinical psychologist. A graduate of the University of Michigan, he received his Ph.D. in Clinical Psychology from Syracuse University. He became an Associate Professor at Eastern Michigan University, a Research and Clinical Psychologist at Michigan's Wayne County Training School. He served in the US Army Air Force (USAAF) from 1942-1946 as an Air Gunner and Radio Operator on Consolidated B-24 Liberator bombers.

Callahan was dissatisfied with the results of traditional psychotherapy. So he began a lifelong quest to find a more effective treatment. One of his favourite quotes was by Sir Francis Bacon, 'God's job is to hide things and man's job is to find them.'

In 1980, Callahan, then aged fifty-five, saw a patient called Mary Ford, who suffered from frequent headaches and terrifying nightmares, both related to her extreme fear of water. She had been going to various therapists for years, with no relief. Dr. Callahan attempted to help her using orthodox treatments for a year and a half when, one day she complained of stomach discomfort as she thought of her fear of water.

To help her, Callahan stepped outside the normal boundaries of psychotherapy and *tapped* under both her eyes with his fingertips, as he knew according to traditional Chinese medicine going back 5000 years, that the stomach meridian passes under both eyes.

To his astonishment, Mary announced immediately that her phobia was gone. She raced down to a nearby swimming pool and began to splash water on her face. No fear, no headaches – all were gone, including the nightmares – never to return.

Realising that our thoughts, subtle energy systems and physical bodies are linked in profound and powerful ways, Dr. Callahan continued to explore and perfect his *tapping technique* which he named "The Callahan Techniques" and have since become known as Thought Field Therapy (TFT).

Setting up the Thought Field Therapy Training Centre in La Quinta, California, during the next thirty years, Callahan aimed to prove to an often sceptical world that this integration of energy and psychology could relieve fears and phobias, craving and addictions, stress related health issues and PTSD with far greater speed and effectiveness than traditional counselling. In doing so, he found immense personal satisfaction through healing countless people around the globe who suffered emotionally and physically.

A student of Callahan's, Gary Craig created a simplified version of TFT called the Emotional Freedom Technique (EFT), which was widely marketed.

Callahan himself demonstrated his TFT tapping therapy on Good Morning America, Phil Donahue, CNN, Regis & Kelly, LEEZA, Oprah, and other television and radio shows worldwide. He published many books including, 'Tapping the Body's Energy Pathways,' 'Stop the Nightmares of Trauma' and 'Tapping the Healer Within.'

Roger's wife Joanne has written of her late husband:

"Roger lived with passion and a zest for living life to the fullest. He had a deep conviction and understanding of the importance of what he was receiving and developing. He persevered against all odds to bring us this gift of healing. He was a true pioneer in a field whose time has now come."

"His gift has profoundly changed the lives and transformed entire regions of traumatized countries—taking them from Trauma to Peace. This will continue to expand across our chaotic planet."

"His work is no longer just about tapping away fear or anger, but about lifting ourselves out of separation and conflict, to a place of love and peace. I have witnessed this evolution and am honoured to be able to help share his gift with a world that so desperately needs it."

I personally will always remain grateful for what, through TFT, Roger Callahan has given me and all the people and pets I have and will continue to share it with. Roger attended the conference where I presented my work in TFT and music. When I received his email to say that he had retired I went into 'writer's block mode' and could not hit the reply button; yes, I know I could have tapped for it. What I did instead was to continue doing whatever I could to bring TFT to more people, *particularly into the world of music*. Roger Callahan was certainly a great man, a genius, as he was first described to me and he will definitely live on with every tap of the hand.

Chapter 35
Judy
(Judith Gabriel née Hutter 1955-2000)

Judy was a past student of Rosh Pinah School (where she would later teach violin for me) and the Jewish Free School (JFS). Her parents wanted her to do science, not music.

The following notes are a copy of a letter I wrote to her husband and three teenage children, when Judy passed away. It reflects and summarises our relationship and different practice regimes.

For Stephen, Zavy, Josh and Lara

This is a tribute to my special friend Judy and some of the memories that I have of her.

We met at JFS, quite possibly in the school orchestra, as Judy was a year older than me. Our love of music brought us together and we spent many happy hours together.

At JYO it was hard for a violinist to begin there and Judy was often in tears attempting to play all the violinists' notes. (As a cellist I guess it was easier to 'fake' things - and fake it I did - especially my vibrato.[1])

At my home we would mostly have egg on toast. We used to get upset with each other. I would practise for ninety minutes and Judy was envious and could not understand how I could do it. Meanwhile I was envious of her completing her practice in just half an hour. I couldn't understand that either!

Judy's home - wherever this was, I followed.

Scotland - and piano duets such as The Queen of Sheba. We had such fun playing these.

Bute - fun

---

[1] I later had to relearn to do a proper vibrato.

Arran - we went youth hostelling and cycling around the Island. We once again argued as I didn't want to sit on the grass (bench only!) and Judy did. The sounds of the seagulls made us cry.

Glasgow - Hi Stephen. I never felt like number three. Soon I was Maid of Honour!

Bristol - Hi Zavy

USA - Hi Josh

London - Judy was Rosh Pinah's first violin instrumental teacher. We were colleagues.

Hi Lara, who would sit quietly during concerts.

Zavy remembers her cello lessons with me at that time.

Bournemouth - I accompany Judy on Suzuki pieces.

We saw each other on holiday trips or short breaks and spoke on the phone every few months. Whenever we did it was as though no time had passed in-between.

Through Judy's Suzuki studies (an internationally known method of teaching music) and me learning hypnotherapy, we came to have new interests that we could discuss.

During her illness, which she bore so bravely, she wanted to hear positive talk. She was always looking towards the future. I last spoke to her on her birthday and she died the day after my birthday.

Judy's passing is a great loss to me. As much as I miss her, often feeling that I am gong through this life on my own, I will always cherish our friendship. It was like no other.

As they say, music speaks louder than words and until her memorial concert, I hope the above will suffice.

CHAPTER 88
Fine
(Pronounced fee'-nay)

When I asked my ninety-five year old mother Josie what message she would like to give readers, she said, "Keep practising!"

'If music be the food of love, play on.'

Rosemary

For further information about talks and workshops contact the author. www.RosemaryWiseman.com

Appendices

Appendix 1
Thought Field Therapy (TFT) Procedures

STEP 1 Scale your problem (SUD scale) 1-10

Think as clearly as you can about your problem throughout and follow the appropriate treatment sequence below. Tap firmly, five to ten times on each treatment spot.

Anxiety/ Stress/fear	Simple trauma	Peak Performance	Anger	Pain
Under eye e	Eye brow eb	Under arm a	Tiny finger tf	Gamut spot x5(
Under arm a	Under eye e	Collarbone c	Collarbone c	Collarbone c
Collarbone c	Under arm a			
	Collarbone c			

STEP 2   Scale your problem (SUD scale) 1-10

Carry out the 9 gamut procedure: Tap the gamut spot on the back of the hand (two centimetres behind the little finger and ring finger knuckles) steadily whilst carrying out the following procedure. For each step allow five to ten taps before moving on to the next one.
1. Eyes closed...
2. Eyes open...
3. Look down to one side (head kept still)...
4. Look down to the other side...
5. Rotate the eyes in a circle...
6. Rotate the eyes in a circle in the opposite direction...
7. Hum a few notes of any tune...
8. Count from one to five out loud...
9. Hum a few notes of any tune.

STEP 3
Repeat STEP 1.

If your distress or upset has now gone carry out the Floor-to-Ceiling Eye Roll:
Keep your head fixed in a level position looking straight ahead. Roll your eyes vertically downwards to look at the floor. Begin tapping the gamut spot and while doing so slowly roll your eyes vertically upwards (over a period of about ten seconds) until you are finally looking at the ceiling. Then stop.

No change or some change but the problem is not completely gone?
Focus on your problem (or what remains of your problem) once again and tap the Psychological Reversal (PR) spot on the side of your hand twenty times. Then repeat STEPS 1-3.

Still no change?
Focus on your problem (or what remains of your problem) and tap your upper lip just beneath your nose twenty times and firmly massage the "sore spot" on the upper left side of your chest in a circular motion ten times. Then repeat STEPS 1-3.

Still no change again?
Contact a TFT practitioner, such as Rosemary Wiseman, for advice - a new aspect of the problem may have emerged which requires a different treatment. Further information can be found online at www.RosemaryWiseman.com

Appendix 2
TFT Treatment Points and accepted abbreviations

Abbreviation
SUD=Subjective Units of Distress

Abbreviation	Point	Location
e	under eye	2cm below the eye
a	under arm	10 cm under armpit
c	collarbone	2cm down from notch in throat and 2cm to right and/or left
eb	eyebrow	where it meets the bridge of the nose
tf	tiny finger	on thumb side of finger nail
if	index finger	on thumb side of finger nail
oe	outside eye	side of eye
mf	middle finger	on thumb side of finger nail
th	thumb	on side of thumb nail on side opposite fingers
sh	side of hand	midway between wrist and base of little finger (same as PR spot)
g	the gamut spot	On back of hand between knuckles of little finger and ring finger 2cm towards wrist
un	under nose	under nose in centre of upper lip
ch	chin	in the cleft between the chin and lower lip

g50	gamut spot	tap gamut spot 50 times
9g	9 gamut procedure as on TFT procedure sheet	
Sq	repeat tapping sequence prior to 9g	

****

Easy way to Learn the 9g (nine gamut procedure)

Tap the gamut spot continuously to the tune of 'Frere Jacques'

1. Close your eyes…
2. Open your eyes…
3. Look down right…
4. Look down left…
5. Circle eyes one way…
6. Circle them the other way…
7. Hum…
8. Count…
9. Hum.

Appendix 3
TFT Treatment Points

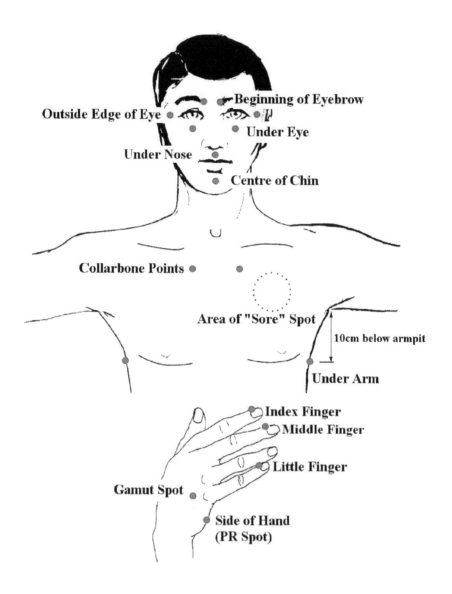

Appendix 4

The Collarbone Breathing Exercise (CB2)
You may need to do this as part of your TFT treatment

Go to the base of the throat (tie knot position). Now go down 2cm and 2cm to the left. This is one collarbone point. Now repeat this process for the right side.

Breathing Positions
There are five breathing positions in this exercise:
1. Breathe normally.
2. Take a deep breath **in** and **hold** it.
3. Let **half** that breath **out** and **hold** it.
4. Let it **fully out** and **hold** it.
5. Take a **half** breath **in** and **hold** it.

Then once again breathe normally!

The Touching Positions
1. Take the first two **fingertips** of the **left hand** (L.H.)
   Touch the **left** collarbone point.
   Tap the gamut spot[1] on the back of the hand continuously while going through the five breathing positions.
2. Place (L.H.) **knuckles** on the same collarbone point. Repeat tapping and breathing positions.
3. Place (L.H.) **fingertips** on the **right** collarbone point. Repeat tapping and breathing positions.
4. Place the (L.H.) **knuckles** on the same collarbone point. Repeat tapping and breathing positions.

Now repeat the Steps 1-4 using the opposite hand and collarbone points.

You have now completed collarbone breathing.

---

[1] The gamut spot is on the back of the hand 2cm nearer the wrist than the knuckles of the little finger and ring finger knuckles.

Appendix 5
Happy Tappers

Happy Tappers
tap away,
any old time
of night or day.
They put their trust in TFT,
(that's short for Thought Field Therapy).
It gives you the tools
that you can use
to calm you down,
to ease the blues.
It gives you freedom
from distress,
it helps to conquer anxiousness.
It helped me in a time
of need,
to gain control,
to plant new seeds.
So thank you Dr. Callahan
for developing your TFT,
it helped to free
my mind of knots,
unwind some tapes,
undo some blocks.
This system Dr. Callahan
shows me a way to say
'I can'!

© Angela Michaels

Appendix 6
Brief notes on Music Students helped by
Thought Field Therapy (TFT)

This article, written by the author, was published in the Thought Field 2004.

Typical PR examples shown in musical performance
These are available from the author, on manuscript paper. The examples would typically involve confusion relating to reversing of clefs; up or down regarding direction of pitch; sharps or flats; left hand or right hand; sequencing of letter names, particularly going down ('backwards') from C.

Sight-Reading
Sight-Reading Psychological Reversal (PR) mistakes in the left hand (sometimes right hand) include the examples as above. PR often shows up in the area of sight-reading because there has been no prior practice of the particular piece and therefore no self-correction of reversals have taken place before or during the 'performance'.

Other musical problems helped with TFT
These include lack of agility of fingers, keyboard geography, rhythmical or co-ordination problems and issues with soloists not giving visual cues to their accompanist to co-ordinate the performance.

Summary
The students or performers are often confused as to what is causing their difficulties and after correction of PR, or tapping TFT sequences, they find the playing easier and feel calmer or more relaxed. In some situations they may not even realise that their fingers are now going to a different and correct note after treatment.

I have helped many music students get good results using TFT or TFT VT with Dr Colin Barron for emotional problems such as guilt, frustration, anger, fear and trauma, as well as toxin identification and treatment (see below). This has improved their performances.

Music exam preparation

The following are brief notes of case studies of music students who I used TFT with to help them prepare for aural (ear) tests for Music Examinations.

I often have a very short amount of time to teach students to sing in tune or be able to clap in time to music. The speed and effectiveness of TFT makes this possible.

PR problems showed on singing tests involving up or down - high or low in pitch.

Once PR was corrected or the seven-second treatment or tapping sequences were given, the student would be able to sing in tune or the pitch would then be accurate.

TFT has also been very useful for helping with students emotional problems in the aural tests, such as by giving them tapping sequences to overcome embarrassment, fear and anxiety. In some cases, treating for embarrassment enabled the student to sing in tune without practice or further instruction.

Case studies involving toxins

The following cases are those where Individual Energy Toxin identification was used either with TFTdx or TFT Voice Technology (VT).

PR mistakes were evident and were corrected without musical practice after doing the seven-second treatment or after avoiding the identified toxins.

Case no.1 Alzheimer's and Rheumatoid Arthritis

I observed PR mistakes with left hand notes. The student or client felt that they were not making progress. Note that piano practice at home was not done at any stage.

They had anxiety and depression, partially as their doctor told them that they 'had lost all their memory'. After toxin identification and avoiding chocolate, eggs and foundation (make-up cream), there were no PR mistakes and it enabled the student to improve emotionally as well as with agility of fingers, ability to use correct fingering, keyboard geography and ability to read music due to improved eyesight.

Case no.2 Multiple Scleroses (MS)

After avoiding the identified toxin of milk, finger work and agility was much improved.

Case no.3

I was having trouble with one student helping them with rhythm in performance. Their parents did not want me to use TFT with them. Coincidentally, their dentist advised them to stop consuming sugar as it was causing dental problems. Since then, the student has had no rhythmical problems on the piano.

Due to me being able to recognise PR through their musical performance, I usually know myself, *before* confirming with the student, whether they have avoided the identified toxin.

Other cases of effective toxin treatment:

Various, including confectionary, sugar, chips, hair gel and deodorant.

Conclusions

Through recognising PR and other problems in musical performance, the potential of the musician can be realised and in so doing, their emotional and physical health, together with their academic ability can also improve, as well as their musical performance.

One parent's comment before using TFT: "Shall I stop the piano lessons as my child is finding it difficult?"

Thanks to TFT and its developer, Dr Roger Callahan, I feel I have become a more able music teacher.

Appendix 7
Look after you voice

Voice abuse is quite common.
These suggestions and exercises will help you with vocal care.

Avoid
1. Shouting – no upstairs or downstairs conversations, screaming or cheering.
2. Clearing your throat. Cough only when you must, and then do it gently and easily.
3. Talking in noisy places, above loud music.
4. Talking when you have a throat infection.

Speak only when others are quiet. Keep in good health.

For all breathing exercises below, use **Diaphragmatic breathing.**

Do the following exercises regularly:
Breathe in slowly for three counts and out for three
Tense and relax shoulders
Rag doll: slowly bend over as if you were a rag doll. Bring yourself up very slowly as if you were controlling a string puppet.
Turn your head very slowly from side to side
Allow yourself three huge yawns
Breathe out – now breathe in, stretch your arms upwards and yawn. As you breathe out put your arms slowly to your side.

Sounds
Breathe in. As you breathe out, make and listen to these sounds:
SS_____(hissing sound)
SS SS SS (Let the air out in three portions)
SS getting louder and then getting softer like a wave.
SH getting louder and then getting softer like a wave.
HUM_____(until you feel a tickle, as your lips vibrate)
Then in the same breath out, make the loud sounds of
MA or ME or MOO or MAW.

Breathing
Breathe in for three, hold for three and then breathe out for three.
Breathe in for four, hold for seven and then breathe out for eleven.

Mirror
Look in the mirror. See that your shoulders are relaxed. To test this, tense and relax your shoulders.

Slow down speech
Take a few breaths in and out. Then do the following SLOWLY:
Count from one to twenty; say the days of the week and months of the year.
Read aloud, record and listen.

Expression
Using any word you like:
Speak in a happy, sad, angry or scared way.

Relax
Tell your feelings to someone. This can help you to feel more relaxed. Relax in a bed or on a comfortable chair. Tense and then relax each muscle in your body. Breathe in through your nose and out through your mouth.

1. Make a circular movement with your feet
2. Wiggle your toes
3. Tense and relax your shoulders three times. Keep breathing while you do this.
4. Breathe out, now breathe in, raise your arms (yawn) and breathe out as you lower your arms.
5. Turn your head very slowly from side to side.

Appendix 8
Peaceful Days

Peaceful Days

Appendix 9

Before leaving Malorees Junior School, our music and class teacher, Mrs Cobb, gave us this poem to write down in our autograph books:

"Thinking" Aka "The Man Who Thinks He Can"

If you think you are beaten, you are;
If you think you dare not, you don't.
If you'd like to win, but you think you can't,
It's almost a cinch you won't.

If you think you'll lose, you're lost;
For out in the world we find,
Success begins with a fellow's will;
It's all in the state of mind.

If you think you're outclassed, you are;
You've got to think high to rise.
You've got to be sure of yourself before
You can ever win a prize.

Life's battles don't always go
To the stronger or faster man,
But sooner or later the man who wins
Is the one who thinks he can.

— Walter D. Wintle

Appendix 10

Weekly Rhythm Record - WRR

Date w/c	Mon	Tues	Wed	Thurs	Fri	Sat	Sun	Total mins.	Goal	Signed

Date w/c = week commencing

222

Appendix 11

Sight-Reading Record Chart

Name _____ Grade _____

Piece Number	Keep Going	Key Signature	Rhythm	Dynamics	Articulation	Tempo	Correct Notes

223

Appendix 12

SUCCESSIPE - Music Practice Successipe Chart

Say Play	Zoom	Slowly	TS	Bits	HS	BP

Zoom - aka 88 model lesson
TS = Time Savers
HS = Hands separately
BP = Basic Practice

Lightning Source UK Ltd.
Milton Keynes UK
UKHW040055190321
380569UK00013B/59